Praise for *The Kid's Guide to Social Action*

"A tremendously useful, well-organized, and inspiring book!"
—Children's Television Workshop

"A wealth of information for kids who want to change things."
—*ALA Booklist*

"The liveliest practical civics book for young students in print."
—Ralph Nader

"If you've been wondering about how to prepare future leaders of our nation, here's a place to start."
—*School Library Journal*

"A great handbook that paves the way for successful, meaningful community projects orchestrated by kids."
—*Chicago Sun-Times*
(Book Week)

"If you want to change the world and are wondering how, grab a copy of *The Kid's Guide to Social Action*. . . . You can make a difference."
—*Kids' Wall Street News*

Awards received by *The Kid's Guide to Social Action*

"Best of the Best for Children"
—American Library Association

"Outstanding Children's Book, Reading-Magic Awards"
—*Parenting Magazine*

"Books for the Teenage Selection"
—New York Public Library

"Children's Book of Distinction Award"
—*Hungry Mind Review*

Seen On

CBS "This Morning"
CBS "Raising Good Kids in Bad Times"
CNN "Newsroom"
CNN "Headline News"

THE KID'S GUIDE TO SOCIAL ACTION

How to solve the social problems *you choose*— and turn creative thinking into positive action

Barbara A. Lewis

Edited by Pamela Espeland and Caryn Pernu

free spirit PUBLiSHiNG®

Works for kids™

Library of Congress Cataloging-in-Publication Data
Lewis, Barbara A., 1943–
     The kid's guide to social action: how to solve the social problems you choose—and turn creative thinking into positive action/Barbara A. Lewis; edited by Pamela Espeland and Caryn Pernu—[Rev. and updated ed.]
     p.   cm.
     Includes bibliographical references and index.
     Summary: Resource guide for children for learning political action skills that can help them make a difference in solving social problems at the community, state, and national levels.
     ISBN: 1-57542-038-4 (pbk.)
     1. Social problems—Handbooks, manuals, etc.—Juvenile literature. 2. Social action—United States—Handbooks, manuals, etc.—Juvenile literature. 3. Political participation—United States—Handbooks, manuals, etc.—Juvenile literature. 4. Problem solving—United States—Handbooks, manuals, etc.—Juvenile literature. [1. Social action. 2. Political participation. 3. Politics, Practical] I. Espeland, Pamela, 1951– . II. Pernu, Caryn III. Title.
HN65.L442   1998
361.2—dc21   98-11036
                                      CIP
                                      AC

Printed in the United States of America
10 9 8 7 6 5 4 3 2 1

Cover design by David Meyer
Cover illustration by Lisa Wagner
Cover photography by Phillip Mueller
Book interior design by Wendy J. Johnson
Illustrations by Steve Michaels

Free Spirit Publishing Inc.
400 First Avenue North, Suite 616
Minneapolis, MN 55401-1724
(612) 338-2068
help4kids@freespirit.com
www.freespirit.com

"Kids in Action: Jackson Elementary" is based on an article by the author which originally appeared in *Sierra Magazine*, March/April 1989. "Ten Steps for Taking Social Action" originally appeared in *Free Spirit: News & Views on Growing Up*, Vol. 3, No. 4, March/April 1990. Ideas for the brainstorming forms on pages 177–178 were inspired by the Talents Unlimited Model, Mobile Country School System, and the Future Problem Solving Model, Laurinburg, North Carolina. The survey forms on pages 185–187 are adapted with permission from "Bill of Rights Newsletter," 8, number 2, page 4, Constitutional Rights Foundation, Los Angeles, California, 1974. Much information on grants is based on *A Citizen's Guide to Community Education*, The League of Women Voters Education Fund, Washington, D.C., 1988, pages 35–53. "Kids in Action: Audrey Chase" is courtesy Dave Block, KLS-TV News, Salt Lake City. Much information on state governments, including the State Legislature Contacts chart on pages 149–150, is from *The Book of States*, the Council of State Governments, Lexington, Kentucky, 1996, and is used with their permission. Much information on resolutions is from "How to Write a Resolution," page 3, from *Study Guide for "How To,"* courtesy the Utah Association of Women Executive Board, Salt Lake City, Utah, 1985. The photo of the KAP kids on page 134 is courtesy *U.S. News & World Report*. "Steps for Mediation" on page 143 is reprinted with the permission of Educators for Social Responsibility ©1997 by Educators for Social Responsibility, Cambridge, MA.

To kids everywhere.
May you be both *seen* and *heard*.

And to Larry, a man of action, who knows
how to get things done.

CONTENTS

CONTENTS

CONTENTS

CONTENTS

LIST OF REPRODUCIBLE PAGES

Special thanks to my publisher, Judy Galbraith, for believing in me, and in the abilities of kids to create social action.

Thanks to my editors, Pamela Espeland and Caryn Pernu, for patience, encouragement, cheerfulness, and fine editing skills

A special recognition to Olene Walker, the Salt Lake Education Foundation, and Chevron USA, Inc., for their support of my initial grant in Community Problem Solving, and to Project 2000 Kidspeak for encouragement.

I have gleaned much information and instruction on teaching critical thinking skills from many individuals, a few of whom I would like to recognize as having especially influenced my thinking:

- The International Future Problem Solving Program, for inspiration and stories;

- Sydney Parnes and Alex Osbourne, for the original Creative Problem Solving Model, which combined critical thinking with action in an understandable way;

- SLC District Media Center, for expertise on the Internet and email;

- Calvin Taylor and the Talents Unlimited staff in the Mobile County Public School System, for their marvelous program for teaching kids to think creatively;

- Joseph Renzulli, for his Triad Model; Barbara Clark, for opening new vistas of what the brain can do; Sandra Kaplan, for her thematic approach to teaching and differentiated curriculum.

Hats off to all the children and their parents in the Extended Learning Program at Jackson Elementary, and to all the other kids and their advisers who have contributed stories to this book.

For believing in young folks, a special thank you to all the community groups, educators, legislators, administrators, and officials who have supported the Jackson children in their projects; and to my principal, Pete Gallegos, and Salt Lake School District for the courage to allow freedom and flexibility in my program.

And lastly, a special kiss to my husband, Larry, and children, Mike, Andrea, Chris, and Sam, for their patience, inspiration, and continued love.

INTRODUCTION

Have you ever been sprawled on the carpet, munching chips, while watching a TV reporter discuss a problem in the news? You may have said to yourself, "I know what I'd do if I were in charge." You saw the solution clearly—somewhere between the time when you dipped a chip in the salsa and crunched it between your teeth. And yet, you wondered, who would listen to you?

You might be shocked at the number of people who would not only listen to you, but also act on your suggestions. Kids around the world are tackling mountains of community problems. And adults are standing with hands on hips and gaping mouths as they witness kids pushing through laws,

cleaning up vacant lots, collecting a billion tons of newspapers to recycle, even making pets out of endangered protozoa. These aren't superkids with magical powers. They're regular kids, just like you.

The Kid's Guide to Social Action can help you transform your creative thinking into actions that make a difference in your neighborhood, your town or city, your state, your country, and your world. And it's written for kids so even adults can understand and use it. But this isn't a book of lesson plans. It isn't a book of ready-made projects. It won't tell you what to do. It *will* give you the skills you need to solve the social problems you choose.

HOW TO READ THIS BOOK

You can dip your toes and wade through different sections, or you can dive in and swim from cover to cover. It's up to you. But it may help to know that this book is divided into five main parts.

PART ONE: LIFE BEYOND THE CLASSROOM

Meet the kids from Jackson Elementary School in Salt Lake City, Utah, whose efforts resulted in the cleanup of a hazardous waste site, the passage of new laws, the planting of hundreds of trees, sidewalk improvements, and anti-crime efforts. Learn how you, too, can create projects that make a difference.

PART TWO: POWER SKILLS

Master the social action skills you need to accomplish your projects. Learn how to write letters, search the Internet, create surveys, pass petitions, picket—even get TV coverage and raise big bucks. You'll see samples of student work and pictures of real kids in action.

PART THREE: WORKING WITH GOVERNMENT

Grown-ups aren't the only ones who can change laws or have an effect on our court system. Kids are doing it, too. Learn how to lobby—how to convince your legislators to vote for your bill. Read about some exceptional kids who are serving as jurors and judges in youth courts.

PART FOUR: RESOURCES

This part points you toward more information—important telephone numbers and addresses and Web sites, groups you may want to join, places to apply for awards, and more. Learn who to call, where to write, and how to get the recognition you deserve.

PART FIVE: TOOLS

Petitions, surveys, news releases, and resolutions—these are just some of the tools of social action. In this part, you'll find the forms you need to put your best foot forward. They're ready for you to photocopy and use.

Throughout *The Kid's Guide to Social Action,* you'll read about other action "bench pressers" who have accomplished everything from cleaning up hazardous waste sites to building a school for child laborers in Pakistan. You'll meet Amber Lynn Coffman, who mobilized kids across the nation to join her Happy Helpers for the Homeless organization, and Porfue Xiong, who volunteers as a translator for Asian immigrants navigating the U.S. health care system. Some kids, like the Conflict Busters in Franklin, Nebraska, are working on projects to improve their school; others, such as Kids Against Pollution, are working on an effort to amend the U.S. Constitution.

All of these kids are heroes. But they're also ordinary kids who just want to design a better future.

If you have a social action story you'd like to share about yourself or someone you know, write it down and send it to:

Barbara Lewis
c/o Free Spirit Publishing Inc.
400 First Avenue North, Suite 616
Minneapolis, MN 55401

If possible, include a telephone number where you can be reached. Your story may be used in future books or articles.

SOCIAL ACTION: WHAT'S IN IT FOR YOU?

> "Parents can only give good advice or put [their children] on the right paths, but the final forming of a person's character lies in their own hands."
> **Anne Frank**

Social action includes those things you do that extend beyond your own home and classroom into the "real world." These things aren't required of you. You don't *have* to do them. You do them selflessly, to improve the quality of life around you.

The real world is chock-full of real problems to solve: real letters to write, real laws waiting to be made, real surveys to analyze, real streams needing monitoring, scraggly landscapes in need of artistic attention.

Isn't it exciting for you that all these problems haven't already been solved? Could you think of anything more boring than growing up in a world where every-thing had already been done, and there was nothing left for you to do?

Solving social problems will bring excitement and suspense into your life. Instead of reading dusty textbooks and memorizing what other people have done, you'll create your own history with the actions you take. And here's a promise to you: As you reach out to solve problems in your community, you'll be helping to design a better future. You'll also be learning to take charge of your personal life. You'll become more confident in yourself, because you'll prove to yourself that you can do almost anything.

WHY SHOULD YOU CARE?

This is the Age of the Kid. The world needs to see your work and to hear your voice. And *you* need to start asserting and enjoying your rights.

Think about it. There have been many social movements to define and strengthen adults' rights. For example, you've probably read about the women's rights movement. Before it got started and grew strong, many people thought that women weren't smart enough or interested enough to take social action, do certain kinds of jobs, even vote in elections. Other rights movements are working to increase opportunities for people who have long been discriminated against. There's an animals' rights movement underway.

But what about *kids'* rights? For years, kids were told to be "seen and not heard." That's not so true anymore. Or is it? Has your country ratified the United Nations Convention on the Rights of the Child? This treaty is the first binding international agreement to set minimum standards to protect the full range of human rights for children—civil and political rights, as well as economic, social, and cultural rights. As of 1997, only two nations have yet to ratify this convention: Somalia and the United States.

Does your community listen to kids? Are kids represented on local committees or school boards where you live? Do your senators ask your opinions before making or changing laws?

Do you find it insulting that most adults think you're only interested in video games and loud music? Are you tired of adults making most of the big decisions that affect your life? Kids are probably the most *un*represented group in the world. Now, some adults might disagree and say that your parents represent you. But there was a time when women were told that their husbands represented them. What's the difference?

No one can represent you better than you. You have a fresh view of life. You don't know all the reasons why something *won't* work. You're willing to try new things. You come up with new ideas. And you have your own opinions.

But your opinions won't be presented to the public unless *you* get out there and do it. Of course, you'll still want to schedule a few video games in between, and take time for music and other things you like to do. When you start working for social change, you don't stop having fun.

Maybe you're not interested in solving *big* problems. That's okay. There are many ways to make a difference, and *The Kid's Guide to Social Action* will introduce you to quite a few. If you're one of those kids who wants to change the world, this book is for you. Or if you're just one of those kids who gets the uncontrollable urge to stand up in a movie theater and shout, "I've had it with the next person who throws an empty popcorn cup or sticky wad of gum on the floor!"—this book is for you, too.

·········▶ Check It Out ◀·········

To find out more about the United Nations Convention on the Rights of the Child, contact UNICEF:

UNICEF
333 East 38th St.
New York, NY 10016
(212) 686-5522
http://www.unicef.org/

CREATE YOUR OWN FUTURE

Whereas,   You are capable of thinking and solving real problems, you should not allow adults (or anyone else) to put you down. Don't pay attention to those who say you can't succeed if you're poor, uneducated, or disabled, or because of your ethnicity, sex, or youth. Don't get trapped by those chilling excuses. They can make you numb. You *can* succeed.

Whereas,   You can make a difference in the world, don't listen to those who insist it's too late to breathe fresh air, control neighborhood gangs, save the rain forests, save the whales, combat drug abuse, and create world peace. It's only too late when *you* stop believing in the future.

Whereas,   You can find your own problems and design your own solutions, be suspicious of anyone who "gives" you a problem to solve or wants you to resolve a pet project. Decide what *you* want to work on, and then invite others to join *your* team.

Whereas,   You should *not* feel responsible for solving all the world's problems while you're still a kid, neither should you feel excluded from creating solutions. Don't be swayed by people who say you're "too young," that you should spend these years dreaming and just being a kid. Remind them of how it feels to be powerless. They will remember. The ability to solve problems doesn't belong just to adults—and the ability to dream doesn't belong just to kids.

Whereas,   You have a right to shape your future, don't wait for someone else to do it for you. Speak up. Speak out. Design a world you want to live in. Don't wait for luck to create it. Luck is just another word for work. The world needs to see your works and to hear your voices. *Now, therefore, be it*

RESOLVED   That this year and every year shall be proclaimed as:
THE KID'S YEAR FOR SOCIAL ACTION
for all kids who believe in themselves, each other, and the future. Don't *allow* life to happen. *Make* it happen!

SIGNED AND SEALED this ____ day of _____.

_____

Signature

LIFE BEYOND THE CLASSROOM

KIDS IN ACTION

Courtesy Paul Barker, *Deseret News.*

Jackson kids survey the neighborhood surrounding the barrel site.

Jackson Elementary

Salt Lake City, Utah. Black dots representing possible hazardous waste sites were sprinkled across the large wall map of Salt Lake City like flecks of pepper. I had hung the eight-foot map on the blackboard so my students could see it easily. They discovered that one of the sites was located just three blocks from our school.

"That old barrel yard?" 11-year-old Maxine asked, shocked at how close the site was to us. "Kids climb all over those barrels!"

"I bet there are at least a thousand barrels in one pile," added Chris. He grabbed a marking pen and circled the spot.

We were studying the importance of groundwater, the underground liquid cities pump up for people to drink. We had learned that hazardous waste can leak down to contaminate the water. I had planned the unit for my academically talented sixth graders at Jackson Elementary, where I teach special classes of fourth through sixth graders. I had no idea I was unleashing a tiger.

As it turned out, Chris had underestimated: The site held 50,000 barrels that at one time had contained everything from molasses and flour to dangerous chemicals. Now, after a recycling business had stockpiled them for more than 40 years, many were rusted and corroded. Residues left in the barrels had long since dribbled out onto the hard dirt.

As the sixth graders threw themselves into finding out if the barrel yard had contaminated the groundwater, the fourth and fifth graders caught their enthusiasm. We now had 34 kids tackling the problem. This was as exciting to them as unraveling a mystery, since it was *their* neighborhood.

I made preliminary phone calls to the health department to alert staff that students would be calling to ask what they might do to help. "There's nothing children can do," one health department official told me. "They'll be in high school before they see any results."

When the kids called health officials, they were shooed away like pesky flies. But since I teach students to solve problems, they didn't give up. They just looked for new solutions.

Their next idea was to conduct a door-to-door survey of the neighborhood, informing residents of the dangers of hazardous waste and searching for wells so they could ask health officials to take water samples.

These two strategies didn't work, either. Surveying a four-block area that included several abandoned houses and warehouses with wooden planks slapped haphazardly over jagged window glass, the children discovered only a few wells, all cemented over. But what surprised them more was the "I don't care" response of the locals.

Before returning to school, we paused outside the barrel site fence. Covering three blocks, the steel mountain of drums blocked the children's view of a community sports arena, the Mormon Temple, and the Wasatch mountains in the distance.

"Look," Maxine said, pointing. "Some of the barrels are orange and yucky."

"Rusted," Chris said.

"And some have big holes."

"Corroded," Chris corrected.

"Look at all the orange color in the dirt," Heather said, "and black, too. I wonder if anything leaked out of the barrels?"

Maxine bent down. "The fence has lots of holes in it," she said. "Bet I could climb through one."

The "protective" fence sagged in spots like stretched-out potbellies. In a later survey of the school's students, 32 children would admit to having played on the barrels.

While we were at the site, some of the kids decided to stop at the barrel yard's office. A worker told the kids to bug off, that there weren't any problems at the site.

But my kids weren't convinced.

To learn more, they began reading articles on hazardous waste in such magazines as the *New England Journal of Medicine, Newsweek, and U.S. News & World Report.* Sound like hard reading? You're right. But the kids devoured the articles, because they wanted answers to their problem.

An environmental consultant, health officials, and Salt Lake City's emergency hazardous waste cleanup team came to our class to lecture. Health officials said that even one cubic inch of dangerous

chemicals could leak down through the soil and contaminate groundwater.

Shauna called the Environmental Protection Agency (EPA) national hotline to ask for help. Other students wrote to the agency's regional office in Denver. Another called the local power company, which owned the land where the barrels were stockpiled.

TV and radio stations and newspapers covered the story of the students' quest.

But things didn't start changing at the barrel yard until the students visited Palmer DePaulis, mayor of Salt Lake City at that time. Luckily for the kids, the mayor had been a schoolteacher. He listened to them. Then he amazed them. He promised to work toward getting the mess cleaned up within 18 months! The kids struggled to walk instead of run out the door.

Once outside, they slapped hands and showed off with a few flips and cartwheels on the front lawn.

Within a few weeks, changes began at the barrel site. Under all the public pressure from people the children had contacted, and the coverage in the media, workers started removing the barrels.

In early June, 1987, just a few months after the kids had begun their campaign, researchers from the Denver EPA office came to Utah to check out the site. Although the sixth graders were enjoying their graduation party, many chose instead to scramble over to the barrel site to watch the EPA dig wells to check the water.

The kids came in dresses and pressed pants, straight from the dance. The girls twirled around,

Jackson kids at the barrel site, where 50,000 barrels were stockpiled. Some contained residues of hazardous waste.

Courtesy Paul Barker, *Deseret News.*

catching the breeze in puffed-out skirts, then arm-wrestled with the boys. Heather won.

"We did it!" they shouted.

Results of the test were promised within nine months.

While the Kids Waited

The kids were proud of their work, and they waited anxiously for the test results. But their pride faded when they learned that the owner of the barrel yard had suffered a heart attack and was in intensive care at a hospital. To make it worse, one of his workers said that the pollution dispute had probably helped to cause his heart attack. "Don't you know that this man has contributed thousands of dollars to the local children's hospital, Little League teams, and other charities?" the man scolded. "We're not contaminating anything. By recycling, we're cleaning up the environment."

If you're confused, so were the kids. They learned that things are seldom all right or all wrong. They thought about this through summer recess. They leaned on the fence by the barrel yard and watched the removal of the barrels by truck and train. The piles shrank. Bare patches appeared on the dirt. Within a year, all the drums would disappear, leaving only the stained soil behind.

In the meantime, I received three phone calls from an anonymous man (not the barrel yard owner) threatening legal action if the kids persisted on the project. Nothing ever came of the threats, but the school district promised legal help if we needed it.

When the kids returned to school in the fall, I expected them to have given up their hazardous waste crusade. After all, how interesting can "garbage" be? I was wrong. Even the old sixth graders (now mature seventh graders) returned to brainstorm new strategies with the younger children.

Some of the kids were still concerned about the barrel yard owner. Was it really their fault that he was in the hospital? Did winning always mean that someone else had to lose?

I called the barrel yard and learned that the owner was in stable condition.

"Who besides you has rights that need to be protected?" I asked my students.

"The barrel yard owner," Chris said. "What's going to happen to small business owners like him who can't afford to clean up their messes? They could lose their businesses, and then only the big guys would be around."

Heather jumped up. "But we have a right to know what's in that dirt. We're living by it."

The other children agreed with Heather.

"Then who should be responsible for cleaning up hazardous waste?" I asked.

"Maybe the health department," one child said.

But a spokesperson for the health department had already told us that their agency didn't have any money.

"Let's earn some money to help everyone, like small businesses and people like us," someone suggested.

"And give it to the health department," another added.

"Let's clean up all the hazardous waste in the state!" Kory suggested, swinging his arms and knocking a stack of magazines to the floor.

"Get real," Chris jeered. "That would cost too much."

But they didn't give up the money idea. They held a white elephant sale and sold all their old mini-cars, doll furniture, and games. They raised $468.22—probably about enough to clean up one square foot of toxic mess.

Heather, always the philosopher, remained optimistic. "It's okay," she said. "It's a start."

The Results Are In

By Christmas, the long-awaited EPA test results came in. Heather tore down the hall, waving a large manila envelope. "The health department just brought this to the office and asked for me!" Her cheeks glowed.

We flipped through the pages together. The report indicated that harmful chemicals, solvents, coal tars, pesticides, and heavy metals had polluted the soil and groundwater at the barrel site. It listed such substances as benzene, toluene, lead, zinc, and copper. Translation: Both the groundwater and soil were polluted.

We didn't know it then, but the site would soon be recommended for the Utah National Priorities List. This meant that it would be given top priority for cleanup. Because Salt Lake Valley drinking water is collected from several sources and mixed, our neighborhood toxic waste site threatened over 477,000 people!

The Next Step ························➤

Although the kids had won that battle, they didn't stop there. They mailed 550 letters to businesses and environmental groups, asking for donations for hazardous waste cleanup. Including the money they chipped in themselves, the students raised about $2,700. They wanted to give it to the health department to help clean up polluted sites.

But they couldn't. The law wouldn't let them.

"Let's just change the law then!" Kory said, punching his fist in the air.

The kids had read about the national Superfund, designed to help clean up abandoned toxic waste sites. Utah had no such fund and ranked near the bottom of all the states in environmental programs. So the students worked together to initiate Utah's first Superfund law for cleanup of hazardous waste. The kids called the legislators on the phone and testified before a legislative committee and the Utah Senate. They passed out flyers to all the legislators, trimmed in red crayon.

On the day of the vote, the kids sat on plush couches at the State House, trying to look grown-up and proper. They crossed their legs and folded their hands—but within two minutes, they were bouncing on the cushions. Then they rushed to the window. In the distance, they could see the barrel site where it had all begun almost a year before.

The lawmakers passed the bill without one vote against it. Because they weren't allowed to clap in this formal setting, the children grinned, mouths open in silent cheers, arms waving wildly.

"No one has more effectively lobbied us than these young kids," one senator said. "And they didn't even have to buy us dinner."

"These children did something we couldn't do because Superfund is such a political issue," said Brent Bradford, a director in the health department. "They've raised the level of awareness of the whole valley to hazardous waste issues."

The kids were invited to speak at universities, education seminars, and community groups. They were featured in many national magazines and newspapers, and received over 25 local recognitions and nine national awards. One of the kids' dads built a trophy case for the front hall of Jackson Elementary to show off their awards.

Passing On the Spirit

But that wasn't the end of the Jackson kids' story. When the original kids went on to junior high, new children came up with projects of their own. They graduated from garbage to sidewalks and trees. Another project brought $10,000 worth of sidewalk repairs into their neighborhood, and the kids have campaigned for more neighborhood improvements.

Like many other kids' groups across the nation, the Jackson kids turned their focus to trees. They learned from the University of Michigan's *Forestry Update* that a single tree, in its average 50-year lifetime, will contribute $62,000 worth of air pollution control. Dubbing themselves "Leaf It To Us," the younger kids decided to think big and applied for two city grants—money to use for their tree planting.

One day Audrey Chase, a fifth grader, had an idea. "Why don't we find money and make our own grants for kids all over the state to plant trees?" The Jackson kids contacted the governor, the state forester, and national forestry people. With the help of Richard Klason, state forester, they found some national money for grants for children in Utah.

Not to be outdone by previous Jackson hotshots, the new kids tackled the legislature again. This time, they pushed through a law creating $10,000 for grants for kids in Utah to plant trees. The law has been renewed every year since 1990. Over $175,000 worth of trees have been planted by kids in the state.

The children brainstormed even bigger ideas. They worked with Utah Senator Orrin Hatch to create a national fund for trees. The kids circulated a petition and collected 1,500 signatures from kids around the nation to support their idea. Audrey flew to Washington, D.C., to deliver the petition and to lobby senators in person.

Although Congress didn't write a special bill for the students, legislators inserted the idea to make money available for kids to the America the Beautiful Act of 1990 (technically called The Food, Agriculture, Conservation and Trade Act of 1990—S2830). This money was dispersed to all the states and made it possible for kids and youth groups to apply for federal grants of money to improve their neighborhoods.

The Legacy Continues

This legacy of social action has continued at Jackson Elementary. A few years later, students decided to fight crime in the area. They surveyed the school and found out that one-fourth of the children had been chased with knives or weapons and that one-fifth of the kids or their family members had been threatened with guns in the area. They discovered that the kids thought the three worst crimes in the area were drugs, gangs, and child abuse.

Armed with this information, the kids went to work. They gave speeches and hosted an anti-crime night with their parents. They lobbied the police department and got their help in measuring off a Drug-Free School Zone and painting over graffiti.

Inspired by earlier Jackson kids, the new group successfully lobbied for three tough anti-crime laws in the Utah legislature, making stiffer penalties for graffiti, drive-by shootings, and possession of weapons near schools.

One day the kids discovered that across the street from Jackson, a house had become a head-quarters for drug dealing. The kids got mad. They wrote letters to the city complaining about it, and city officials ordered the house to be bulldozed. The children then helped build a new low-cost house for a family. Patrice giggled and said, "Just think—I helped build this house."

Hearing stories of child abuse, Jackson students decided they needed to work to make life safer for kids. They worked to amend a child-abuse law, allowing teens to be trained to advocate for abused kids in court. They wrote a public service announcement for TV, and also had the slogan put on a billboard. Written by Moleni and illustrated by Andrea, the billboard read: "You always lose if you choose to abuse."

After several years of trying, the kids finally realized a dream to create a hotline for kids who had been abused or wanted information about child abuse. It was hard. "Lots of people told us why it wouldn't work," Amanda said. Many people turned them down. Finally, their principal, Marilyn Phillips, suggested that they apply for a grant. They followed her advice and got the hotline, as well as 25,000 stickers displaying the phone number—enough for all the children in the Salt Lake City school district.

What Can You Do?

Now, you're probably saying something like, "Yeah, but those Jackson kids are hotshots. I'm just a regular kid. I can't do all that." If you're a disbeliever, let me assure you. I'm their teacher, and I'll tattle on them. They sometimes forget assignments. They lose papers. Their bedrooms aren't always clean. They're kids just like you, kids with dreams, kids who care. They're not rich or unusually clever. In fact, their school has had the lowest income per capita (per person) in the Salt Lake City school district.

But one thing they do have is courage. They don't give up easily. They're interested in the future, because they plan to live there. They're not afraid to tackle hard things that other people say can't be done.

As Heather said, "Big things happen in small steps."

> "Whatever you do may seem insignificant, but it is most important that you do it."
> Gandhi

10 TIPS FOR TAKING SOCIAL ACTION......➤

> **"Luck is a matter of preparation meeting opportunity."**
> **Oprah Winfrey**

You've read about the Jackson kids. Anything they can do, you can do, too. Here are ten steps that will lead you to your goal.

1 Choose a problem. Look around your neighborhood. Are there any areas that look neglected or need improvements? Are there places that make you feel unsafe? Places that smell awful? Any problems with drugs, crumbling buildings, homeless people, hungry children, dangerous street crossings, grungy landscapes?

This is one good way to begin. You could also find a problem by thinking about a subject you have studied at school or in a scout troop. For example, if you have just finished a unit on mammals, you might ask yourself, "What kinds of problems do animals have or cause in real life?" If you can't think of anything, you might call your local humane society, animal shelter, or research clinic.

The hard part won't be finding a problem. (For some suggestions, see page 16.) The hard part will be choosing only one problem at a time.

2 Do your research. If you choose a problem from something you have studied at school, you already have valuable information to use. But try some new ways of researching, too.

Survey your school or neighborhood to find out how other people feel about the problem you want to tackle. Telephone officials for information, then interview them over the phone or in person. Write letters. Read magazines and newspapers. Check out the Internet to find information or allies. If you happen to be a veteran couch potato, flip the TV to a news channel.

In Part Two: Power Skills, you'll learn more ways to do research.

3 Brainstorm possible solutions and choose one. Think of what you might do to solve your problem. Brainstorm everything you can think of. Sometimes the zaniest ideas turn out to be the best.

After you have made a long list of potential solutions, look at each one carefully. Choose the solution that seems the most possible and will make the most difference. For example: We will help young people learn to read by volunteering as tutors in the elementary school; we will help reduce crime in our area by organizing a neighborhood watch program.

4 Build coalitions of support. A *coalition* is a group of people working together for the same goal. Find all the people you can who agree with your solutions. Survey your neighborhood; ask teachers, city officials, newspapers, legislators, other students. Call state agencies that deal with your problem. Send email to connect with businesses and nonprofit organizations interested in your issue.

This is *very* important to do. Organize all these people. The more people you have on your team, the more power you will have to make a difference.

5 Work with your opposition. For every good solution, there are people, businesses, and organizations that might oppose the plan. That's why it's important to ask, "Who or what might make it hard to carry out our plan?" It's important to identify possible barriers before you run into them. You don't want to be taken by surprise. Brainstorm with your coalition of support to help you identify who might object to your solution. Teachers and other experts can help as well. Then make plans to overcome others' objections.

You might be tempted to think of the people who oppose your solution as "bad guys." But it can be more useful to see them as people with different needs and opinions. Get to know your "enemy"; you might be surprised how far you can get by working together, and how many ideas you agree on. Not all the time, but in many cases, you and your opposition can both win—or at least accomplish more by compromising.

6 **Advertise.** Here's good news: Television, radio, and newspaper reporters love stories of kid action. TV and radio stations usually offer free air time for worthy projects.

Call and ask to speak to a reporter who covers educational issues. Or you might write a letter. Be sure to include a phone number (yours?) the reporter can call for more information. Or send out a news release.

Don't forget small community newspapers, even church bulletins. They can help you advertise, too.

If you let people know what problem you're trying to solve, and what solution you propose, you'll suddenly find all sorts of people who want to climb aboard.

7 **Raise money.** After letting people know about your project, you might try to raise funds to support it. This isn't essential, and many wonderful projects can be tackled without this step. But sometimes you have more power if you put money where your mouth is.

8 **Carry out your solution.** You have your lineup of team players, and you've advertised to let people know the problem you plan to solve. Now DO IT!

Make a list of all the steps you need to take. Give speeches, write letters and proclamations, pass petitions, improve your neighborhood or school (or you might just try to spiff up your own backyard).

9 **Evaluate and reflect.** Is your plan working? Are you congratulating yourself on your coolness, or do you feel more like you have a migraine headache? It's time to evaluate your project and its progress.

Have you tried everything? Should you change your solution? Do you need to talk with more people? It's up to you. You're in charge.

Reflect on what you've learned. What have you actually accomplished? Write, draw, or dramatize your experiences; express your reactions to the service you have performed in an imaginative way.

10 **Don't give up.** Unless *you* think it's time to quit, don't pay too much attention to folks who tell you all the reasons why your solution won't work. If you believe your cause is really important, keep picking away at it.

Problem solving means weeding out all the things that don't work until you find something that does. Remember, a mountain looks tallest from the bottom. Don't give up. Climb!

WHAT'S YOUR PROBLEM?

Maybe you already know a problem you want to solve. Or maybe you're truly stuck on finding an issue to pursue.

On page 16, you'll find a list of areas from which you might brainstorm a problem. But first, let's review the Four Rules of Brainstorming:

1 Brainstorm with a friend, your family, a group, or a class. The more brains you have to storm with, the more ideas you'll have. But you can also brainstorm alone.

2 Everybody tries to come up with as many ideas as possible—from silly to serious, and everything in between.

3 All ideas are acceptable during brainstorming. Write all of them down now, and make your choices later.

4 Nobody criticizes anybody else's ideas. Period. No exceptions!

You can brainstorm on blank paper, a chalkboard, a flip chart, a computer, or anything you choose. On this page and the next, you'll find examples of two filled-in brainstorming forms. The first is for writing down ideas. The second is for choosing an idea to work with, then making a plan of action.

If you like these forms, you'll find blank ones on pages 177 and 178 that you can copy and use.

BRAINSTORMING I: COME UP WITH IDEAS

That makes me think of: / **more WILD & crazy ideas—Keep going**

idea - ideas

pollution
air land garbage water

→ factory stacks
car exhaust
— dioxin gas masks
solar powered cars
scrubbers on stacks

→ drinking water
hazardous waste
— lead in water pipes
midnight dumping
bacteria, germs

→ landfills
— fertilizer

idea - ideas

broken up sidewalk

→ sidewalks missing-
8th West
— walk in streets
elderly trip and get hurt

→ lack of city money

→ neighbors don't care
— people move away too fast

idea - ideas

grafitti drugs
abandoned buildings vandalism

→ gangs
the old paint factory
— railroad station hides it
dropouts

→ the corner at 6th West
night time
— lights broken or missing

→ neighbors don't watch
— don't know each other

·········· BRAINSTORMING II: CHOOSE YOUR MAIN IDEA ··········

At this point, you have many ideas, some of them crazy. Now you should choose an idea to work on.

Ask yourself questions.

For example:　Which idea might make the biggest difference? Which idea might have the best chance to succeed? Which idea might benefit the most people? Which idea might cost the least to do? Which idea do I like the best?

QUESTIONS

1. Which idea might be the most possible to do?

2. Which idea do I like the best?

3. Which idea might help the most people?

4. Which idea might cost the least for us?

5. Which idea might help us learn the most?

Choose one basic idea to work with:

We will encourage sidewalk repairs in the Euclid area

Now list the steps to carry out your Plan of Action.

For example:　Give speeches at the community council. Write letters to the mayor. Write a news release for TV and radio.

Then write down who will be responsible for each step, and when.

PLAN OF ACTION

Activity	Who Does It?	When
Photo survey of sidewalks	All of us	March 10
Call City Council	Gwen	March 7-11
Write speeches	Gwen, Sara, Donny, Dung, Errin	March 12-13
Speak to Mayor and City Council	Gwen, Sara, Donny, Dung, Errin	March 18
Call engineers	Sara	March 19
Write news releases	Donny, Errin	March 19
Meeting with engineers	All of us	March 30

WHAT'S THE PROBLEM? ◄ ··

Unfortunately, problems in need of solutions are easy to find. Reading the newspapers, watching the news on TV or listening to the radio, surfing the Web, reading books or magazines, or talking to people in your school and community can all help you identify problems that need to be tackled.

Here's a list of topics that might get you jump-started. Ask yourself, "What's the problem?" for each of these topics. Decide which ones you might want to work with, or brainstorm topics of your own.

Community Concerns

Schools
City growth and development; land use
Vacant lots, abandoned buildings
Beautification projects
Animals and wildlife
Libraries
Literacy
Parks and recreation
Sports and athletics

Social Concerns

Families
Child care
Friends and social relationships
Population
Immigration
Diversity
Clothing
Homelessness
Public health, mental health
Nutrition and hunger
Substance abuse (alcohol and other drugs, smoking)
Volunteerism
Support systems for children, the elderly, etc.
Poverty
Employment, unemployment

Governing Agencies

Transportation
Law enforcement and justice
Education
Business and labor
Lawmaking agencies and governments
Social agencies
Elections and voting
Court advocacy

The Environment

Energy production, energy use
Natural resources
Wildlife
Hunting and fishing
Pollution (air, water, land)
Weather
Garbage and recycling

Technology

Communication
Information access
Satellites and space research
Medical research
Industrial advances
Inventions and projects
The future of technology and space

Value Systems

Money
Economic growth
Human rights
Children's rights
Ethics (morals and beliefs)
Religion
Censorship
Trade
Working conditions

Public Safety

Peace
Weapons and gun control
Safety and accidents (including industrial)
Terrorism
Disasters (earthquakes, floods, fires, storms, etc.)
Disease
Crime

KIDS IN ACTION

Around the World

"Activism pays the rent on being alive and being here on the planet. . . . If I weren't active politically, I would feel as if I were sitting back eating at the banquet without washing the dishes or preparing the food. It wouldn't feel right."
Alice Walker

You can start taking social action in your own back-yard or neighborhood, but you don't have to stop there. Many kids are literally changing the world. Around the world, young people are participating in international meetings to improve the environment, to promote peace, and to improve rights and conditions for all children.

Scout groups everywhere have been busy tackling community problems. In Fiji, scouts turned a piece of neglected coastal land into a beautiful green space for local people and tourists to enjoy. Others in Indonesia re-greened an area serving over 25,000 villagers after it was devastated by a fire. In Central Java, scouts constructed a pipeline to bring fresh water for drinking and for watering rice fields to more than 11,000 people in four different villages. And in the Netherlands, scouts and local politicians joined to organize 25,000 scouts for a tree-planting project in 500 European cities.

Scout troops aren't the only young people who are making a difference worldwide. A group of Swedish school children began an international effort to save the Costa Rican rain forest. In Zambia, one young volunteer organized a troupe of actors to perform anti-poaching plays in different villages. He wanted to discourage the wasteful killing of animals for their skins and for fun.

Kids in the Marshall Islands are applying for grants to get better playground equipment. Youth in Argentina, Uruguay, and Paraguay have helped to plant trees, paint a school and hospital, and clean up parks, streets, riverbeds, and orphanages. A young girl in South Africa planted 150 trees along the streets of Atteridgeville. In the Galápagos Islands, a boy raised funds to improve his neighborhood by designing badges and selling them.

A Toronto student, Craig Kielburger, was inspired by a 12-year-old Pakistani youth who toured North America to make people aware of the millions of children enslaved in his country and others. Young Craig traveled to Pakistan to investigate the conditions in person and then organized an international campaign to free children from forced labor.

Students at Sunnyside Elementary in Marysville, Washington, have adopted a stream, helped save salmon, and formed a partnership with a sister school, Ligura Elementary, in Tokyo, Japan.

Does it make you tired just reading about the things these kids are doing? Or does it light a fire under you? If you're one of the fireballs, you can join with the thousands of kids who are working for a better future.

"It's a small world, but I wouldn't want to paint it."
Stephen Wright

SNIFFING OUT SOLUTIONS
KEEP YOUR SENSES ABOUT YOU ◄·········

Once you've brainstormed and decided on a problem to solve, you can begin your research. Research doesn't have to be boring—especially when you're working on a cause you care about. Make a game out of your search and go on an old-fashioned scavenger hunt to sniff out possible solutions to your problem. A scavenger hunt is a game in which you try to find items on a list within a certain time limit. The person or group that comes back at the end with the most points wins.

If you don't want to have one group project, you can divide up and do small group projects, or work individually. (This activity also works well when searching out problems.)

These questions can help guide you on your search for solutions:

SNIFFING OUT SOLUTIONS SCAVENGER HUNT

- You may work with other students, teachers, parents, club members, or alone. If you're working on a group project, decide whether to play the game as individuals or divide into teams.

- Set a reasonable time limit for your search.

- Copy the form on page 179 to track your progress. List the names, phone numbers, addresses, and Web sites of people, organizations, businesses, and other sources of information.

- Select awards for the winners—the teams or individuals that accumulate the most points.

1. **What frustrates you?** Do you see ways of reducing your problems so that things run more smoothly?

2. **Do you see ways to reduce your problem to improve safety for people or things?**

3. **Research your problem using the Internet, newspapers, magazines.** What information can you find? What new resources do you discover?

4. **Interview experts on all sides of your issue.** Keep your mind open to all new ideas. You can do this in person, by letter, email, or phone. What resources support your ideas? Who might offer different solutions? Who might build roadblocks in your way?

5. **Use your senses:** Listen to what's said. Look for new ideas. What do you observe? Do you see ways to fix your problem? Improve it? (Have you checked under, behind, and around things?) What do you hear, see, and smell?

6. **What do your hunches tell you after you've spoken to experts?** Go through your list of solutions and cross off any that won't work.

7. **Choose the solution that will help you reduce your problem the most.** See the Brainstorming II form on page 178. Ask yourself these questions as well.

You might even find people ready to join your team to form a coalition. Be sure to check out the Power Skills in the next section to help you hone your telephone, letter writing, email, and interviewing skills!

Scoring Guidelines ◄···················

___ **One point** for every resource you identify.

___ **Two points** for each phone call, letter, or email to a possible resource.

___ **Three points** for each personal interview you conduct.

___ **Five points** for making an appointment with someone to talk to your class or club.

___ **Ten points** for enlisting a promise of help from an agency or person.

___ **TOTAL**

EVALUATE & REFLECT

What happens when you complete a project? What do you do next? Move on to something else?

Before you put your accomplishments behind you, it's a good idea to reflect on your experience, to evaluate your project, and to assess how well you met your own goals.

Not taking time to evaluate your experience is like ignoring the pieces of a puzzle scattered across your carpet. When you think back on your project, you put the puzzle pieces together and get a more complete picture of what you've accomplished. Evaluating and reflecting help you to understand what you learned. You discover different angles of looking at your experience. And you can do it many times—after your project, and even before and during your project.

A written evaluation can be an added bonus. You may be able to use this evidence of your experience to get credit for a project with your teacher, a club, or your scout or religious leader. Years later, you can refer to your project when applying for a job, a special camp, a scholarship, or even a college program. You'll probably impress your teachers, parents, and other adults around you. Most of all, when you write an evaluation, you record what you did so that you can never forget it.

TIPS FOR WRITING AN EVALUATION

1 **Describe the problem or issue.** *Example:* Some children in second grade are not reading up to grade level.

2 **Describe your research.** *Example:* I surveyed the teachers in the school to find out who needed help. The teachers gave me teaching materials to use. I read an article, "How to Tutor Kids in Reading." And the second-grade teachers tutored us on tutoring.

3 **Describe your solution.** What service or project did you do? Tell the details about what happened. *Example:* I spent one hour a week reading with a second grader. We picked out books to read together and took turns reading out loud to each other.

4 **Tell who you helped.** List the contact names, phone numbers, and addresses of the people or organization you helped. This is important so you can reach these people again. It also gives someone else a way to continue your project.

5 **List everyone who helped you on your project and what they did.** *Example:* Fred Bilcow collected pencils and paper from teachers. Melinda Yang talked to the faculty with me. Mr. Washington gave pointers on tutoring.

6 **Describe your time line.** (How long did you work on your project?) List the dates and hours of service you provided. This is important to document what you did. *Example:*
- October 1—Melinda, Fred, and I decided we wanted to help kids learn to read.
- October 3—Fred collected materials and Melinda and I talked to the teachers and librarian to get permission. Mr. Washington said that he had three students who needed help.

- October 10 to October 20—Mr. Washington gave us lessons on tutoring.
- November 1 to April 30—I read books with Lucia for 20 minutes on Mondays, Wednesdays, and Fridays.

7 **What skills did you develop or learn?** *Examples:* public speaking, letter writing, listening, research, public relations (getting along with people), computer use, organization.

8 **Reflect on what you learned.** What difference did you make? What might you do differently? What advice do you have for someone else doing your project?

9 **Attach any evidence that you might have collected.** *Examples:* written materials on tutoring, newspaper articles about the project, lesson plans, cassette recordings of kids reading aloud, videos of tutoring sessions. Maybe your evaluation will have many parts and you'll store it in a box.

10 **Share what you have learned.** Find a way to let others know about your project. You just might motivate someone else.

REFLECTING ON WHAT YOU HAVE LEARNED

Thinking about how you can communicate what you've accomplished or learned can enrich your experience. When you reflect, you think about what you've done, decide what you might do differently, process what you've learned, and assess how your solution worked. Reflecting is an ongoing process. Some people choose to create a product as a way of reflecting so they can share their discoveries with others. Presenting your project to others can help you see what you've done in new ways and through new eyes. It can also spark others into action.

How can you reflect on your project and share what happened? The possibilities are almost limitless. You might come up with some wonderful, creative products that you can add to your portfolio and save forever. Here are some lists of ideas to get you started:

Reflecting/sharing through speaking
- Group discussions
- Chants, choral reading
- Panel discussions
- Debriefing
- Debating the issues and problems
- Singing
- Giving speeches
- Conducting Q & A sessions
- Monologues
- Cassette recordings
- Interviews
- Reports
- Chain stories
- Feelings forums
- Presenting research
- Lobbying
- Telephoning
- Representation on boards and councils

Reflecting/sharing through writing
- Journal writing
- Newspaper articles
- Creative writing (poetry, drama)
- Booklets, brochures, flyers
- Public service announcements
- Essays
- Raps, jingles
- Short stories

- Newsletters
- Jokes, cartoons
- Commercials / advertisements
- Chain stories
- Surveys
- Pen-pal writing
- Recipes for good service
- Petitions for help
- Riddles
- Satires
- Timelines
- Tests / quizzes
- Dictionaries
- Diagrams
- Information cards
- Databases
- Field trip plans
- Sharing research
- Proposals
- Proclamations

Reflecting/sharing through art or performance

- Charts, posters
- Animation
- Photography
- Videos
- Drawings / paintings
- Characterizations
- Charades
- Plays, dramatizations
- Improvisations
- Role-playing
- Mime
- Puppets shows
- Skits

- Murals
- Puzzles / games
- Mobiles, models
- Mosaics
- Scrap books
- Overhead transparencies
- Slides
- Illustrations
- Cartoons
- Banners
- Origami
- Quilting / fabric design
- Sculpture
- Crafts
- Etchings, carvings
- Flags
- Dioramas
- Maps
- Parading, picketing, protesting
- Musical performances
- Singing
- Dancing

Reflecting/sharing through math and science

- Statistics
- Story problems
- Survey analysis
- Fundraising
- Experiments
- Games
- Graphs and charts

•••➤

Once you've completed a social action project, you'll have looked at your original problem closely. You'll probably see the issue more clearly that when you started. At this point you might set up a debate in your class, family, or club to challenge everyone's thinking. Or you might decide that you want more people to hear about the issues and, like KidsFACE from Tennessee, write a PSA for a local radio station. Maybe you'll want to create a play for younger kids, like the students from Carl Sandburg Junior High in Levittown, Pennsylvania, who wrote a skit to teach younger children about forest fires.

If you're a more private or artistic person, maybe you'll want to make a poster, mural, or mobile to hang in your own bedroom to remind yourself of your experience.

However you choose to reflect, this process is important. Neglecting to reflect on your experience is like leaving the clay pottery you just made in a soft form that may get smooshed by a careless toss of your schoolbooks. Reflecting is like putting your clay pot into the kiln to achieve a fuller, lasting beauty.

And the most exciting part of social action will be when you look at yourself in the mirror after completing the project. You'll see that you have also been sculpting the clay of your character. If you look closely at your face, you might see new lines of understanding etched there, a more confident sparkle in your eyes, a glow of compassion on your cheeks. Your face will reflect the growth of your character, and that's the greatest gift you can give yourself and others.

> "A small group of thoughtful people could change the world. Indeed, it's the only thing that ever has."
> **Margaret Mead**

Part 2

POWER
SKILLS

POWER TELEPHONING

For many kids, the telephone is essential to a well-rounded social life. But did you know you can also use it to organize and collect information, interview people, take surveys, or even lobby someone? You can save a lot of time if you let your fingers do the walking.

The telephone is one of the most basic communication tools we have, yet telephones in schools are practically kept under police protection. To use them sometimes requires a letter of permission from your parents (or an act of Congress). However, if you're working on a problem at school with other classmates, your teacher can usually get permission for you to use the guarded phones.

If you're not a phone-call veteran, copy and fill out the phone form on page 180 before making your call. This will put many needed facts in front of your nose, like the name of your contact (the person you're calling) and your name. (That's right, *your* name, just in case your brain closes up shop when you get an important official on the phone.)

You'll also have your return address and phone number. Most people know their home address, but if you're calling from your school or club, you may not have that address memorized. If your contacts want to mail information to you, you don't want to be rude and make them wait while you hunt around for an address.

Finally, you'll have written down what you plan to say or ask. And you'll have a place to write down what your contact tells you.

WELL, I GUESS IF I CAN'T USE THE PHONE THE MAYOR WILL HAVE TO CALL ME!

SCHOOL OFFICE

HOW DO I FIND A TELEPHONE NUMBER?

There are many ways to find telephone numbers: (1) your local telephone books or the collection of national and international telephone directories at your local library, (2) Internet telephone directories, and (3) directory assistance.

Finding What You Want in the Telephone Book

- The *blue* pages list government agencies: city, county, state, and federal government offices.
- The *yellow* pages list businesses, associations, clubs, groups, and so on, by category (Conservation Services, Legal Help, etc.).
- The *white* pages list people and businesses by name.

In bigger cities, the white and blue pages may be published in one directory, the yellow pages in another. The color codes might change from city to city. Watch for this if you need to use many different directories at your library to track down your contacts.

Finding What You Want on the Web

If you're hooked up to the Internet, you can always log on for easy access to a number of different directories. Looking for the phone numbers and names of all the radio stations in Chicago? These sites can help you find most U.S. phone numbers and addresses for businesses and residences. Visit the Web site and follow the directions:

WhoWhere? *http://www.whowhere.com*
Four11 *http://www.four11.com*
Lycos *http://www.lycos.com/peoplefind/*
The *Original* Yellow Pages *http://206.141.250.39*

Using Directory Assistance

Okay, your other efforts to get the phone number have failed. You can simply dial directory assistance to get the telephone number you need, but you'll probably have to pay a small fee.

If you are calling a business or organization, one of the best places to try first is the toll-free directory. Dial 1-800-555-1212 to see if the organization your want to reach has a national toll-free number. This is a free call that can save you money in telephone charges.

If you strike out there, call 1 + the area code + 555-1212, and an operator will help you get the number you're looking for. You can usually find a map of United States area codes in the front section of your local telephone book.

TELEPHONING TIPS

1 Get permission to use phones at your home, school, group, or club. It might sound routine, but it's important.

2 Copy and fill out the phone form on page 180. Unless you're a seasoned phone buff, it's good to have that information at your fingertips.

3 When someone answers your call, state your name, grade, and school or organization. Even if you're doing a project on your own, you'll probably get better service if you mention your school name.

4 If you don't know the name of a contact, ask for someone in public relations or public information. This will usually land you in the right department.

5 If your contact isn't there, ask when he will be there. Write down the time. Call back at that time. Or leave your name, grade, school or organization, a phone number, a time when he can reach you, and a brief message about why you're calling. Most officials will return calls.

6 What if your contact doesn't call you back? Be a pest! Call again and again. Persist until you get the information you need, but always be polite. Never speak rudely. It will only hurt your cause. Remember, it's not your problem if someone else is rude. But don't worry. Most officials will think you're terrific.

7 When your contact does answer the phone, tell him your name, grade, and school or organization again. Then move on to the purpose of your call—what you want to say or ask.

8 Write down exactly what your contact tells you. You might have to ask him to repeat things. Most people talk faster than you can write. Even though you may be able to instantly memorize stats on every player in the National Football League, you'll probably forget details of your phone conversation within five minutes of hanging up. So write it down!

9 While you have your contact on the phone, get his correct name, title, address, ZIP code, and phone extension. You may have talked to several people on your way to the right person. Maybe the first person put you on hold, then switched you to another person, who switched you to another person. . . . You don't want to go through that all over again.

10 Leave your name, address, and phone number with your contact. That way he can get in touch with you again.

11 When you have the information you need, thank your contact. Then hang up.

12 File the phone form where you can find it again.

IMPORTANT

Never leave your home phone number or address without permission from your parents.

Courtesy Porfue Xiong

Porfue Xiong

Fresno, California. When the Communists took over Laos in 1975, tens of thousands of Hmong families fled their mountain homes. Young Porfue Xiong and his family planned their escape to Thailand. Terrified of being caught and tortured or shot, they hid in bushes and under jungle canopies during the day and walked silently by the moon's light at night. They were taken into a refugee camp when they arrived in Thailand. The Xiongs lived in camps for five years, waiting for permission to emigrate to the United States. Conditions in the camps were harsh. Porfue feared beatings from the camp guards and not getting enough to eat.

Porfue and his family arrived in California when he was 16. He wanted to give something back to the country that had accepted his family. In the camps, Porfue had become fluent in many languages, including Hmong, Lao, Thai, and Chinese. In California, he learned English quickly, too. During Porfue's junior year at Fresno High School, he began volunteering at a family clinic, translating for immigrant Asians. Many of them had never been to a Western doctor before. Shots and surgery were very different procedures from the traditional herbal cures of their homeland. Not speaking the same language or being able to tell the doctor about their symptoms caused great anxiety.

"It's very emotional to see patients crying because they are so afraid," Porfue said. Porfue allayed the patients' fears as he explained the doctor's procedures to them. He also told the doctor what the patients were feeling. Sometimes the patients would grab Porfue's hand in gratitude. Porfue would look down, catching his breath, always remembering what it felt like to have fear claw at his chest. He also began making phone calls for the doctor to help set appointments and answer questions for Asian families.

During the summer, Porfue answered the telephones at the Fresno Community Hospital, where he worked in the emergency room. Once again, he translated for recent immigrants, called families, and reassured them that the patients were receiving good medical care. He set up appointments for future care.

Porfue explains what his volunteer efforts have meant to him. "I felt I was helping my community by bridging the communication gap. I was able to help the two different worlds understand each other."

POWER LETTER WRITING

Have you ever really thought about what "The pen is mightier than the sword" really means? When it comes to persuading people to action, good writing is better than force. Good writing can change history.

You can have a great deal of power to make a difference in the world if you learn to write effective letters. And the best way to learn is to *do* it.

There are many different kinds of letters. Here are six:

1. **Information letters** gather information or give information to someone else.

2. **Persuasive letters** try to influence someone. For example, you might write to a legislator to ask her to support a bill.

3. **Support letters** thank people or tell them that you agree with them. For example, you might write to a lawmaker to say that you like a bill that he wrote.

4. **Opposition letters** tell people that you don't agree with them. For example, you might write to your governor to say you don't agree with the way your state is spending money.

5. **Problem/solution letters** identify a problem or propose a solution. For example, you might write to a newspaper editor stating the need for a larger zoo, a library, or an improved highway system.

6. **Request letters** ask for someone's help, encouragement, or support for a project.

HOW TO WRITE A LETTER TO THE EDITOR

Imagine how much fun it would be to see your writing in your neighborhood or city newspaper! You can do it. It isn't that hard. Your ideas could reach hundreds of thousands of people in a statewide newspaper—many more in a national magazine. It's a great way to advertise and to make people aware of your problem.

Here are 12 tips for writing a letter to the editor that will enhance your chances of getting published. The two letter forms on pages 181 and 182 will help you to arrange the parts correctly. The form on page 181 shows you what to put where. The form on page 182 is blank so you can copy it and use it for your own letters.

1 **Look for any rules printed in the magazine or newspaper you plan to write to.** (Often these are found at the end of the Letters column.) Or call the newspaper on the phone to ask for special instructions.

2 **Write on school stationery for extra clout.** If school stationery isn't available, use plain white or off-white paper.

3 **Type your letter or write it on a computer if possible.** But don't worry if you can't type or don't have access to a computer. You can hand write your letter, as long as it's neat and readable. Use only blue or black ink.

4 **Include your return address and signature.** Most newspapers and magazines don't print anonymous letters, although some editors won't print your name if you ask them not to.

5 **Start your letter like this:**
To the Editor:
And end it like this:
Sincerely,
(Your signature)
(Your name typed or printed)
(Your grade, school, or organization)

Nothing fancy, nothing mushy, nothing too difficult.

6 **Make sure that your letter is brief and clear.** Come right to the point and don't repeat yourself. Editors aren't impressed with long-winded letters. In fact, letters are often shortened to fit the space available in the newspaper or magazine. Don't be surprised or upset if this happens to your letter. ....➤

"I have made this letter longer than usual, because I lack the time to make it short."
Blaise Pascal

7 **Write timely letters.** Your subject matter should be something that's "in" or of current interest.

8 **Never accuse anyone of anything without proof.** Writing something libelous could get you into trouble. (Libel makes someone look bad unfairly. People can get sued for libel.) Remember: You want to *solve* problems, not be a problem.

9 **Support your solution.** If you're writing because you think something should be done, give a few short reasons why.

10 **Never send an "open letter" addressed to some public official to a newspaper or magazine.** It will probably end up in the editor's wastebasket.

11 **Don't send the same letter to more than one newspaper.** You probably wouldn't appreciate receiving a form letter from a friend. Newspapers like original work, too.

12 **Proofread your letter for mistakes before sending it.** But don't worry; your letter doesn't have to be perfect. The editor will make any needed corrections.

Kimberly Clegg
1469 So. 2000 E.
S.L.C., UT 84108
February 6, 1997

Deseret News
Po. Box 1257
S.L.C., UT 84108

Dear Editor:

I am writing because I think that Downtown Salt Lake City is too full of construction. Every time I go Downtown, I feel like the air is so brown and polluted, because of all the buildings that are being repaired or constructed.

I understand that the buildings must be made, but I think that we could make it a little more clean, by staggering times that these buildings are under construction.

I hope that we can be able to clean up Downtown by the time the Olympics arrive.

Fifth grade student,

Kimberly Clegg

Kimberly Clegg

HOW TO WRITE A LETTER TO A PUBLIC OFFICIAL

Should you write a letter to the mayor, the governor, a senator, even the president? Of course you should, if you have something to say. Follow the tips for writing a letter to the editor on pages 30–31, with these added hints. Copy and use the letter forms on pages 181 and 182 if you need help deciding what goes where.

1 The best time to write to a public official about a specific issue is a month or so before the legislative session begins. She has more time to read your letter then. A week or so after you send your letter, call the official on the phone to jar her memory.

2 Make sure that your letter includes your return address, so the official can write back to you.

3 State your purpose in the first sentence. If you're writing to support or oppose a bill, identify it by number and name at the beginning.

4 Stick with one issue per letter. Don't try to wipe out air pollution, improve the budget, start a light-rail transit system, and save the whales all at once.

5 You probably hate writing assignments that require a certain number of words (you spend more time counting than writing). You'll be glad to know that letters to officials should be as short as possible—only a few paragraphs, at the most—while still getting your point across.

6 It's okay to disagree with a public official, but do it politely. Never write a rude letter, and never threaten.

7 If possible, be complimentary. It never hurts to include a comment about something good the official has done. She'll be more willing to listen to a complaint or suggestion if you start off on a positive note.

8 Don't apologize for taking the official's time. Listening to people—including you—is her job. She might be surprised to get a letter from a kid, but that could work in your favor.

9 If you write to a legislator other than the one who represents your area, send a copy of your letter to your own representative. That's good manners, and your representative may want to help you, too.

You'll find an example of a real letter on the next page.

Jackson Elementary
750 W. 200 N.
SLC Utah 84116

The Honorable Mayor Palmer De
Paulis
The office of the Mayor
324 South State
Salt Lake City, Utah 84111

Dear Mayor De paulis:

We would like to be involved
in repairing cracked and distorted
sidewalks in the Euclid Area.
I would like to see the sidewalks
repaired because of how bad it
makes the Euclid area look, I, Myself
have seen the sidewalks, and they aren't
a very nice sight. My friend and I
were walking down to a park in
the Euclid area And my friend
tripped on some rocks and scraped
her leg up So I would really
appreciate it if the sidewalks
were repaired
            Sincerely,
        Krista Crawford Fifth grade Ely

33

POWER ADDRESSES

Here are some official addresses, plus examples of how you should start and end your letters. If you don't know the names and addresses of your own senators, representatives, governor, and mayor, ask your teacher or a parent, or call your public library.

President of the United States

The President
The White House
Washington, DC 20500
  Dear Mr. President:
  (Or Dear Madam President:)
  Very respectfully yours,

Vice President of the United States

The Vice President
The White House
Washington, DC 20500
  Dear Madam Vice President:
  (Or Dear Mr. Vice President:)
  Very respectfully yours,

Member of the President's Cabinet

The Honorable Madeleine Albright
The Secretary of State
Washington, DC 20301
  Dear Madam Secretary:
  (Or Dear Mr. Secretary:)
  Sincerely yours,

U.S. Senator

The Honorable John Glenn
United States Senate
Washington, DC 20510
  Dear Senator Glenn:
  Sincerely yours,

U.S. Representative

The Honorable J.C. Watts
House of Representatives
Washington, DC 20515
  Dear Representative Watts:
  Sincerely yours,

Governor

The Honorable Christine Todd Whitman
Governor of New Jersey
  Dear Governor Whitman:
  Sincerely yours,

Mayor

The Honorable Sharon Sayles Belton
The Office of the Mayor
  Dear Mayor Sayles Belton:
  Sincerely yours,

  (Use this form for letters to your commissioner, too.)

World Leader

(Name of World Leader)
(Country) Embassy
United Nations
United Nations Plaza
New York, New York 10017

Check It Out

The Address Book: How to Reach Anyone Who Is Anyone by Michael Levine (Perigree Books, updated annually). You can find addresses of famous people, including actors, singers, artists, authors, and CEOs. For all ages.

Also available: *The Kids' Address Book.*

SENDING YOUR LETTER BY FAX

A fax (short for *facsimile* message) is like a cross between a letter and a telephone call. Your message is written in letter form, but it's sent over the telephone lines rather than by mail. The nice thing about a fax is that you can get your message out very quickly. While you might not get an instant reply (as you would if you spoke to someone over the telephone), you can better organize your thoughts and make sure they are clear before you contact a person or organization. There's another advantage, too: You can send diagrams or pictures to help support your viewpoint, which you can't always describe over the phone. Plus, if you send your message by fax, the recipient is more likely to reply by fax—and you'll get an answer quickly, too.

A fax machine is simple to use, and most businesses, government offices, organizations, and schools have one. Many convenience stores and copy centers will send a fax for you for a small fee. You can even send a fax directly from your computer screen if you have the right software and modem.

When you send a fax, you need to prepare you message neatly in letter form, using the letter-writing skills described on pages 30–32. To make sure your message gets to the right person, you should also include the following information on a one-page cover sheet. (You can use the cover sheet form on page 183.)

COVER SHEET

✏ **To:** (the name of the person you are faxing)
Company: (the organization you are faxing)
Fax number: (the recipient's fax number)
Business phone: (you may also add the email address, street address, or any other needed information)

✏ **From:** (your name)
School or organization: (the name of your organization or school)
Fax number: (yours)
Business phone: (your school's phone number. This is very important because you need to make sure that the person can answer your fax! You might also add your email address, street address, or other informtion.)

✏ **Date:**
✏ **Number of pages:** (including the cover sheet)
✏ **Subject:** (what you are writing or asking about)

Check with an adult to get permission to use the fax machine. Ask someone to show you how that particular fax machine operates. In general, you lay your pages face-down in the tray, dial the number of the fax machine you're calling, press the START button, and watch your pages feed through the machine one at a time as they are sent. You usually get a message (either on paper or on the display screen) telling you whether or not your fax was sent successfully. ·····

SENDING YOUR LETTER BY EMAIL

Electronic mail, or email, lets you quickly send out messages to other people anywhere on the planet: to a pen pal in Russia or a schoolroom in Ouagadougou in the African nation Burkina Faso. The only requirement is that you both have the right equipment: a computer and an email account. Instead of licking a stamp and dropping your "snail-mail" letter in the mailbox, you send the message electronically with the click of a button. You can save on postage and make almost-instant connections with other kids who care about the same projects that you do.

Email offers many advantages:

- It's speedy. You can receive an answer as quickly as your friend can read your message and type a reply.

- You can send a letter or document to many people at the same time, without having to use the copy machine or pay for extra postage.

- You can join mailing lists from interesting organizations to receive their newsletters electronically.

- You can research information on your favorite issue by contacting organizations through their email address.

- You can get the latest news delivered right to your computer.

Email Addresses

Internet addresses follow a standard format:

name@organization.extension

The *name* identifies the individual or group that receives the message.

The @ means "at."

The *organization* identifies the company, institution, or service providing access.

The . (called "dot" when you're saying an address out loud) is used to separate elements of the address.

The *extension* offers more information about the type of account. For example, *gov* is used by government offices, *edu* by educational institutions, *com* by commercial businesses, *org* by nonprofit organizations, and *net* by computer networks. This is useful, because it can help you identify who really is providing the information. There's plenty of great information on the Internet, but there's also a lot of garbage. You need to know your source.

Here are some examples of what an address might look like:

president@whitehouse.gov
boots@compuserve.com
lgomez@harvard.edu

Be sure to type addresses very carefully and double-check your typing before you send your message. Even one little mistake or typo can send your message to the wrong person or make it come bouncing back to you with the message that your mail was "undeliverable."

Sending a Message

You might be surprised at how easy it is to use email. Every email program works a bit differently, so be sure to ask someone to show you how to use your setup. It will just take a few minutes before you feel like a pro. Here's how it typically works:

1 Select the command to start a new message. Different programs have different commands, but it will be something like NEW, TO: MAIL, or COMPOSE. When you click on the button or select the command, a new message window will open on your screen.

2 Enter the recipient's email address in the TO box. You can enter more than one address if you are sending a message to several people.

3 Type a brief description of your message in the box that says SUBJECT or RE.

4 Type your message in the big blank box.

5 Send your message by clicking the button that says SEND or OK.

It's even easier to reply to a message. Just click the REPLY button when you're done reading the message. The recipient's address is automatically filled in, so you don't have to look it up and type it in. You can type your response and then hit SEND.

Netiquette (Net Manners—They Matter)

- Don't use rude or offensive words, write bad things about others, or try to get other users mad. Always be polite in your messages, even those you are sending to friends.

  Be aware that email messages are never totally private. Other people—hackers, the administrator of your email account, or people who share your computer—might be able to tap into your account and read your messages. And don't forget that the people you email can forward your words to anyone else.

- Keep your password secret. That's how you protect your email account and your files. Don't give your password to anyone, not even people who claim to represent your online service. They already have access to your password and won't need to ask.

- If you've received a message that you want to forward to someone else, ask permission from the person who sent you the message.

- Never pretend to be someone else in your messages.

- Always give credit to your source when you use information you get from someone by email or through Internet research.

- Be brief. Just as with other letters, when you write to officials by email, get straight to the point.

- Don't use ALL CAPITAL LETTERS because they are considered SHOUTING or having an EMAIL TANTRUM.

- Give your recipient time to respond. Just because you can get your message out quickly, doesn't mean that other people can respond immediately. It might be a few days before they read your message if they are not in the office. Or they might need time to look up some facts, talk to someone else, or think about their reply. Or perhaps they never actually received your message. If a few days pass without a response, send a polite note asking if they received your earlier message.

- Say no to chain mail. Don't send it or receive it. It wastes valuable time and ties up the lines.

- Treat other users with respect.

····▶ Finding Email Addresses ◀····

Okay, so you're ready to send an email, but how do you get the right email address? Usually the easiest thing to do is to pick up the phone and ask! But there are also some handy Web sites that can help you:

Lycos	*http://www.lycos.com/peoplefind/*
Four11	*http://www.four11.com*
WhoWhere?	*http://www.whowhere.com*

POWER INTERNET RESEARCH

Once you have access to the Internet, the a new world of information is opened to you. The Internet is great tool for communication and research. You can find immediate contacts and current information on the problems you tackle. Facts about everything from asbestos to zebra mussels are just keystrokes away. You can also find places to post your information and advertise your cause.

Nobody owns the Internet. Except for the fee you pay your provider, you can travel the information superhighway with very few tolls, charges, or speeding tickets. You can visit most Web sites free, although a few (like the *Wall Street Journal*) ask you to subscribe.

You can research up-to-date information on practically any subject you can think of. Ask a Net-savvy librarian, teacher, or friend to show you what she knows. But in the meantime, here are some tips on how to get started:

VISITING AN INTERNET SITE

When you know where you're going on the Internet and you have an exact address—called a URL (uniform resource locator)—it's easy to pop in for a visit:

- Click into your browser's address box, which is usually near the top of your screen.

- Type in the URL, which will look something like this: *http://www.csg.org/*

- Click the FIND or GO TO button, or hit "return" on your keyboard.

- Wait patiently, and the site will appear (unless something goes wrong, of course, like you typed the address incorrectly).

- When the site's home page comes up, you can click on links (icons or words that are in color or underlined) to get to more information.

SEARCHING THE NET

If you don't have the URL for the site you want to visit—or you don't know exactly where you want to go—you'll have to search. Click into your browser's NET SEARCH box to get a list of Internet directories and search engines. These are the vehicles that guide you through the Web to your information, so you'll want to get to know them.

Directories screen and select the sites they list and offer a short description of each. Directories are good to use when you want to browse to see what information is available. Information is arranged in categories from general to specific. You can start by clicking on a broad category (such as News and Media), and then narrow your search (Magazines, Health Magazines, *Today's Health*). Popular directories include Yahoo!, Yahooligans, and Lycos's A2Z.

Search engines are good to use when you know exactly what information you're looking for. Searching this way can be easy: type a word or phrase into the search field and click on the SEARCH button. You can search by

- typing in a specific site name or organization (New York Times, National Institute on Drug Abuse, UNICEF), or

- typing in keywords that describe what you want (teen courts, lead poisoning).

Your search may result in thousands of responses. The closest matches are listed first, so if you don't find what you're looking for in the first 10 or so, you might want to narrow your search and try again.

Type in new keywords that are more specific, try checking synonyms, or put quotation marks around a phrase to limit your search to that phrase, not each single word. (For example, look for *"water pollution"* rather than *water pollution*.) Practice will make this easier.

When your search finds the site you want, simply click onto your choice and you'll be whisked right to it.

Popular search engines include Lycos, AltaVista, InfoSeek, HotBot, Search.Com, Excite, and WebCrawler.

More Helpful Search Tips:

- Remember that the best matches will appear first in the list.

- On the bottom or side of the Web page, you may find additional links to related information. You can click into any of these.

- Hints for narrowing your search sometimes appear near the top of your search page, especially if you have too many "hits." You can follow those instructions.

- Common words don't make good search words *(you, me, the, need, where, etc.)*

- Try to use specific keywords that point out the differences between information.

- Try another search engine if you don't find what you want.

- Check your spelling if you don't find what you need. If you make a mistake, the Internet search engines won't catch the error for you.

- Sometimes files move, the line is busy, or access is denied. You can try again later or start over.

FINDING INFORMATION YOU CAN TRUST

The Internet provides an enormous amount of information from all kinds of different people and organizations. How do you know what's useful and what's unreliable? Sometimes it can be hard to tell. But here are a few questions you can ask as you do research on the Web:

- *Who maintains this site?* Check the URL and see if you recognize the organization and extension. Is the site written and maintained by the government? a university? a reputable company or nonprofit organization? Or is it an individual's home page? If it's hard to tell, try emailing the webmaster and asking directly. (Web sites usually contain the email address of the person who posts and updates the information.)

- *When was the site last updated?* Just because it's on the Web doesn't mean it's up to date. Have you ever seen a sign for a garage sale fading in the sun because someone neglected to take it down after the sale? Some Web sites are like that. The person who put it up has long since moved on to something else. If you're looking for the most current information available, don't rely on a site that hasn't been updated in months—or even a year. Many sites list the date they were last updated. If the one you're visiting does not, look for other clues—for example, do all the links work? If they don't, the information might be old. Again, you can email the webmaster to ask if you're unsure.

- *Does the information reflect what I already know?* Does the site refer to other sources you know are reliable? Can you see any biases in the writing? Does the site provide in-depth information or does it only skim the surface? Has the site won awards that you recognize? All these things can tell you something about whether a particular site has what you're after.

Use your critical thinking skills when doing research on the Web. When you know where your information comes from, you can be more sure that you've got the facts.

CHAT ROOMS, USENET GROUPS, AND MAILING LISTS

Whatever your cause or area of interest may be—whether it's the environment, rap lyrics, or "The Simpsons"—there's probably a chat room or a newsgroup devoted to your subject. *Chat rooms* offer live conversation with people logged in at the same time. You might be able to chat live with a kid from India or a professor at Yale. *Usenet groups* are newsgroups or bulletin boards devoted to specific topics. People can ask questions or post responses that can be read at any time. *Mailing lists* are discussions you can subscribe to. Messages come straight to your email account. Mailing lists are usually more focused and serious than chat rooms and newsgroups.

Before joining an online discussion—whether in a chat room or on an online bulletin board—it's usually a good idea to "lurk" for a time. Read the postings and observe the unwritten rules of the group. Be sure to read the FAQ (frequently asked questions) file so you know what questions have already been discussed before you joined.

IMPORTANT

Exercise caution online. Don't agree to meet an online friend without adult permission and don't meet anyone alone.

CREATING A HOMEPAGE

Kids all around the world are creating homepages for their clubs, school classes, hobbies and practically anything else you can think of. A homepage allows other Net surfers to learn about your cause or project. (For an example, see Kids in Action: Broad Meadows Middle School, pages 42–43.)

·········▶ IMPORTANT ◀··········

DO NOT POST YOUR NAME, ADDRESS, OR PHONE NUMBER ON THE INTERNET, UNLESS YOU HAVE PERMISSION from your parents and anyone else associated with your project, such as your teacher, club leader, or religious leader. Everyone on the Net will have access to the information you post.

·········▶ Check It Out ◀··········

Creating Web Pages for Kids & Parents (Dummies Guide to Family Computing) by Greg Holden (IDG Books Worldwide, 1997). Explains how to design interesting Web pages and includes a CD-ROM with tools, templates, and clip art.

The Internet for Teachers (For Dummies series) by Brad Williams (IDG Books Worldwide, 1997). This book gives instructions on using the Internet that even teachers (and other Internet novices) can understand.

The Kid's Guide to the Internet, by Bruce Goldstone and Arthur Perley (Troll, 1997). Explains how the Internet works, how to send email, how to use the World Wide Web, how to visit a chat room, and more. Ages 7–13.

Kids Rule the Net: The Only Guide to the Internet Written by Kids (Wolff New Media, 1996). Kids review the Web sites they love the most. Ages 7–14.

Life on the Internet: Beginner's Guide
http://www.screen.com/start/guide/
This site provides information on software, email, Usenet groups, creating your own homepage, connecting to the Internet, resource lists, search tools, and thousands of destinations.

Web 66 International School Web Site Registry
http://web66.coled.umn.edu/schools
This site maintained by the University of Minnesota provides links to schools around the world.

Photos courtesy Ron Adams

Broad Meadows Middle School students

Broad Meadows Middle School

Quincy, Massachusetts. "I kept looking at the scar left from a beating by an overseer," Amanda Loos said. She described Iqbal Masih, the 12-year-old Pakistani boy who was speaking about children's rights to the seventh grade class at Broad Meadows Middle School in Quincy, Massachusetts. Iqbal's growth had been stunted by malnutrition. "When he sat in the chair, his feet didn't even touch the floor," Amanda added.

Iqbal's father had sold the boy into bonded labor with a carpet manufacturer when he was four years old for the equivalent of $12.00 to pay for his brother's wedding. Iqbal was to repay the debt by working for pennies a day. Sometimes chained to the carpet loom, sometimes beaten and abused, Iqbal had worked for 12 to 14 hours a day, six days a week, for six years. At 10, he fled the factory and joined the Bonded Labor Liberation Front to fight against forced child labor and educate child workers about their rights.

Iqbal was visiting the United States to receive the Reebok Human Rights Youth-In-Action Award when he spoke to Amanda's class. He told his story to the wide-eyed seventh graders at Broad Meadows, who had grown up in relative luxury with electricity, waterbeds, and Nintendos. He told them

A school for Iqbal in Pakistan. Over 275 kids attend.

he began giving speeches against child labor and working to free other children because 7.5 million kids under 10 were enslaved in his country (and tens of millions of children around the world). Iqbal held up a carpet tool and a pencil and told them that kids should learn to use pencils instead of carpet tools. All he wanted was to be able go to school.

Enraged, Jim Cuddy said, "I thought that slavery died in Lincoln's time. I had no idea it was still going on in so many countries." He raced home that night and called 60 carpet stores to find out if they were aware that their carpets might have been woven by children in forced labor. All but one told him to mind his own business.

Amanda and her friends Jennifer Brundige and Ellaine Legaspi clicked into the Scholastic Network on the school computer, composed a letter, and emailed it to 36 middle schools across the nation. Their letter told Iqbal's story and asked other kids to work against child slavery.

Iqbal returned to Pakistan, where he received death threats. Four months later, in the spring of 1995, Iqbal was shot to death while riding a bike in front of his grandmother's house.

Broad Meadows kids heard the news and mourned. "I was shocked and devastated, but determined not to be paralyzed by violence," Amanda remembers.

"Iqbal really wanted a school for kids in the Punjab province," one student said. "Let's build his school," they all decided.

The students sent out email messages again, this time asking for donations for "A School for Iqbal." They asked for donations of $12.00 because Iqbal was sold for $12.00 and was murdered at age 12. Volunteers from Amnesty International created a Web site for them.

They received over 3,000 snail mail replies (letters), which they answered by hand, and at least 6,000 email messages. Within a year, they raised more than $147,000 and had teamed up with Sudhaar, a Pakistani group that took over the project of building the school. By November 1996, the school opened and was serving 278 students ages four to 12. All of the children work, but their employers now have to allow different shifts so that they can attend school.

Broad Meadow students set aside a portion of the money they collected as a fund for 50 families to use to buy their children out of labor contracts. Still not satisfied with all they had done, the students offered mini-loans to mothers to start their own businesses so they wouldn't have to sell their children.

According to Broad Meadows teacher Ron Adams, "The kids here have never met the children in Pakistan. This whole project has been done by email letters." Broad Meadows kids are still receiving donations, and they are receiving recognition for their efforts, including the Reebock Human Rights Youth-in-Action Award.

Student Michael Gibbons sums it up: "Iqbal has become a symbol of the lost children in poor countries everywhere. Maybe we should build another school."

··········▶ Check It Out ◀··········

Read more about this story at the Broad Meadows Web site:
http://www.digitalrag.com/iqbal

Scholastic Network, an Internet subscription service, links K-8 teachers and students with other classrooms around the world and provides Internet search tools for schools.
http://scholasticnet.com/

POWER INTERVIEWING

Where do you usually go when you need information? newspapers? magazines? books? the Internet? your library? Those are all good sources, but reading is just one way of gathering information. You can learn a great deal from talking with an expert.

And if you need really current information, an interview is better than a book. Books can take a year or more to produce, but an interview is *now*. Besides, interviewing someone can be fun. It's exciting to chat with a person face-to-face.

There are many different types of interviews. Here are four you can try.

1. **Information-gathering interviews** are fact-finding missions to learn more about your problem.

2. **Personality portraits** help you paint "word pictures" of famous people or experts. What makes them tick? Find out.

3. **Opinion-gathering interviews** are like surveys, but you can find out much more information, and you get to know the person besides.

4. **Persuasive interviews** help you build coalitions of support. Talk about the problem you're tackling. Try to convince the person to help you. You'll have more power if you can convince important people to join your team.

Will your administration make the environment a top priority?

INTERVIEWING TIPS

1 Call or write to set up an appointment. (The phone is faster.)

2 Before the interview, list four or five questions to ask. Other friends or a teacher can help you think of some.

Don't take a whole suitcase of questions to ask. Leave some room in the interview for spontaneous questions and answers.

3 Copy and use the interview form on page 184. Record the name, title, and contact information of the person you'll be interviewing.

Write your questions on the form, and number them. During the interview, write the answers in a small notebook or extra paper. Don't try to write them under the questions on your form—you never know how much space you'll need. Instead, identify your answers with the same numbers you gave the questions.

After the interview, record the date and the starting and ending times.

4 Arrive at the interview on time with all of your supplies—interview form, notepad, and pens or pencils.

5 If you have a tape recorder, you could take it along to record the interview. But you must get permission from the person you're interviewing. And it's still a good idea to take notes, writing down the most important ideas. If your notes are hard to decipher later, you can check the recorder for accuracy. (And if your recorder doesn't work for some reason, you'll have your notes.)

A tape recorder isn't essential. Some people prefer only notes.

6 If you have a camera, you could bring it and snap pictures. Again, you must get permission from the person you're interviewing. If there are products to photograph, this is especially enjoyable.

7 If you're a furious note-taker, double-check to make sure you have enough paper. And plenty of sharpened pencils. (Get the point?)

8 If the person you're interviewing wants to go off on a tangent (in other words, wants to talk about something else besides the answers to your questions), let her. You might get some of your best information that way. But make sure you return to your questions so you get the information you need.

9 Remember that you're there to learn, not to impress the other person with how much you know. Good interviewers are good listeners, too.

10 Ask the person where she learned her information. That's a good way to check on the accuracy of what she's saying. And, of course, ask her where you can go to learn more.

11 If the person speaks too quickly for you to write her answers, politely ask her to repeat what she said.

12 You might want to invite the person to be a guest speaker in your class. Take a calendar along just in case.

IMPORTANT

**Never go alone to an interview.
Always get a parent, teacher, or other
adult to go with you.**

13 Before you leave, thank the person for her time. And when you return home or to school, write a thank-you note and mail it right away. Not only is this polite, it also makes the person more eager to help you again.

14 Organize your interview information in some way and present it to your class, a community council, or some other group whose members might be interested. *Share what you have learned.* This is the step where you can really make a difference.

Check It Out

The Elements of Interviewing by Kenneth G. Shipley, Ph.D. (California State University, 1995). Contains information on what makes an effective interview, how to structure an interview, planning questions, and more.

Courtesy Patricia Naden

Franklin Elementary Community Problem-Solving Team teaching from their conflict resolution workbook.

Franklin Elementary School

Franklin, Nebraska. The kids on Franklin Elementary School's Community Problem-Solving Team were concerned. Ever since the construction of two new school buildings had taken away part of the playground, quarrels and fights at recess had become common. Calling themselves the Conflict Busters, the kids observed what was happening at recess. They noted many students shoving, pushing, grabbing balls, arguing over rules.

"It's sometimes really hard to let things go in class because you're still thinking about the argument," said Jessica Ziegler, one of the ten 11- and 12-year-olds working on the project.

Zack Zade rubbed his blond crewcut. "And kids have a lot less to do when they go outside."

"I really miss the basketball court," added Mitch Bydalek, an avid sports enthusiast.

Their teachers, Marilyn Hayes and Patricia Naden, agreed. Ms. Hayes added, "Approximately 200 kids have to share this same space and equipment."

The Conflict Busters needed information to help them solve the problem. They decided that if kids had consistent rules for the most popular games, the worst conflicts could be prevented. So they prepared questions and interviewed teachers to get information. They used what they learned to write a rule book for the school. Now everyone would follow the same rules. They also wrote a conflict resolution book with worksheets for every grade.

Next they interviewed an artist-in-residence who helped them plan playground improvements. Then they interviewed the superintendent to find out what equipment was allowed on the playground. They were disappointed to discover that the school had no money for new playground equipment.

Did the kids give up at that point? Certainly not! They took their project to the city council, who listened to their problem and then designated some lottery money for a new basketball court. The kids cheered, especially Mitch.

"I was surprised that the adults would listen that much to us," said Karsen Zade.

And the kids surprised the adults with their politeness—not only during the interviews, but also with their thank-you notes and appreciation later.

⋯⋯⋯▶ Check It Out ◀⋯⋯⋯

Franklin Elementary School's Community Problem-Solving Team is affiliated with an international organization, the Future Problem Solving Program (FPSP). Find out more about this dynamic group:

Future Problem Solving Program
2500 Packard Rd., Suite 110
Ann Arbor, MI 48104-6827
(313) 973-8781
1-800-256-1499
http://www.fpsp.org/

POWER SPEECHES

Do your palms get clammy at the mere thought of giving a speech? Or are you one of those kids who automatically migrates to the microphone to monopolize it? Either way, you can learn to give great speeches. You might be surprised at the attention officials will give to your ideas.

TIPS FOR SUCCESSFUL SPEECHES

1 **Choose the right audience to hear your speech.** These should be people who would naturally be associated with or interested in the problem you're tackling—and people who have power to act on your ideas.

2 **Remember KISS (Keep It Short and Simple)?** It works for letters, and it works for speeches, too. Short speeches are usually more powerful and memorable than long ones. One to four minutes is plenty.

> **"A speech does not need to be eternal to be immortal."**
> **Muriel Humphrey**

3 **Keep your speech from sounding "canned."** After you finish writing it, jot down one or two words to remind you of each sentence or paragraph. Make a list of these words to take with you. (You can sneak a peek at these if you get a brain cramp when you're giving your speech.) Memorize ideas, not whole sentences.

Here's an example:

If your written speech says this:	*write down and remember this:*
With all the air pollution we have in our city, trees can be a big help. One tree, in its average 50-year life, will clean up $62,000 worth of air pollution.	air pollution 1 tree = $62,000
Cars contribute to air pollution with exhaust. Sometimes it seems like there are more cars on the road than there are people. Industrial stacks can pollute the air, too.	exhaust industrial stacks

4 **Practice delivering your speech.** Practice by yourself at first, until you feel comfortable. Deliver it to a wall. (Walls make very quiet audiences and hardly ever talk back or criticize.) When you feel more secure, practice with a friend or family member.

5 **Will you be nervous before giving your speech?** Probably. Most people chew their nails down before getting in front of an audience. Since you're a kid, however, no one will expect your speech to be perfect. And when you deliver it, just imagine that you're talking to your family and friends. It will help you to speak in a more natural way.

6 **Look at your audience when you speak.** Keep your chin up and smile. The most important thing you have to sell is yourself.

7 **If you're interrupted by noise, stop.** Wait until it's quiet before starting to speak again.

8 **It may seem to you as if you're shouting into a megaphone, but speak loudly and slowly.** If you speak into a microphone, hit it dead center with your voice.

9 **Make your speech interesting.** Tell a story, describe an experience, quote an expert, shock your audience with a statistic. You may want to show slides, a video, a chart, or a graph. If you use any of these things, make sure they're big enough for the whole audience to see.

10 **Leave time for questions and answers at the end.** Five or ten minutes should be enough.

11 **Hand out a one-page flyer.** Listing the major points of your speech can help you impress your audience. And you may want to leave a phone number where you can be reached for more details.

⋯⋯► Check It Out ◄⋯⋯

Speaking Up, Speaking Out: A Kid's Guide to Making Speeches, Oral Reports, and Conversation by Steven Otfinoski (Millbrook Press, 1996). Strategies and encouraging tips for making speeches of all kinds. Ages 11–14.

Toastmasters International
P.O. Box 9052
Mission Viejo, CA 92690
(714) 858-8255
http://www.toastmasters.org/
An organization founded to help people speak more effectively. Contact your local Toastmasters Club to see if it's willing to conduct a Youth Leadership program for you and your friends. The program lasts for eight sessions, and you'll need at least 10 participants, ages 13–16. Regular Toastmasters clubs are open to people ages 18 and up.

What! I Have to Give A Speech? by Thomas J. Murphy and Kenneth Snyder (Grayson Bernard Publishing, 1995). How to organize a speech, use humor, control nerves, and gain confidence and professionalism. Ages 12–14.

KIDS IN ACTION

Photos courtesy Bobbie L. Coffman

Amber Coffman presents gifts to the homeless.

Amber with some of the homeless she has helped.

Amber Lynn Coffman

Glen Burnie, Maryland. Amber Lynn Coffman likes to talk. She's one of those kids who feels as comfortable with a microphone in her hand as she does with an ice cream cone. Amber got hooked on speaking and service at age nine when she did a book report on Mother Teresa. She loved speaking about her hero, and was further inspired after volunteering in a local homeless shelter.

Amber started Happy Helpers for the Homeless when she was 10. Using her persuasive speaking ability, she has presented at many organizations, clubs, and businesses to convince people to donate to her cause. At Christmas, she hosts a huge gift drive. In the spring, Amber and her volunteers hand-stuff 300 Easter baskets for children and adults. She includes toiletries such as combs, brushes, and soaps. The Salvation Army allows her to use their building as a center for many activities, including coat drives and arranging for haircuts, dental treatment, and job help.

Every week Amber and her volunteers—usually about 14 kids a week, ages four through 18—prepare 600 bag lunches in her apartment. Her patient mother watches as the kids form an assembly line across the carpet. Now Happy Helpers has incorporated and thrives in 30 or more states, providing services for the homeless.

Amber's efforts have not gone unnoticed. Written up in numerous magazines and appearing on Nickelodeon and "The Today Show," this dynamic young woman has been recognized by The Giraffe Project as a young hero willing to stick her neck out. In 1995, Amber received the Young Adult National Caring Award. In 1996, she was selected to carry the Olympic Torch to symbolize "Hope for the Homeless." In 1997, she received the Prudential Spirit of Community Award and was honored at the Presidents' Summit for America's Future. Crayola has named her an "Ultimate True Blue Hero," donating $10,000 to Happy Helpers for the Homeless and putting her name on a new crayon.

Comfortable whether she's speaking to a handful of people or to a crowd, Amber spoke to 1,000 young people on National Youth Service Day about being involved in community service. Amber says, "It's indescribable when you speak in front of a group. You introduce new ideas to people, make them aware of the issues out there, and get them involved. I get a warm, fuzzy feeling inside."

What does Amber want to be when she grows up? A broadcast journalist, of course.

Check It Out

For more information on Amber Lynn Coffman and other young people who've started ventures to help the homeless check out Youth Venture's Homelessness & Hunger Web page:

http://www.youthventure.org/html/homelessness_hunger.html

POWER SURVEYS

A survey is a collection of information that gives you a broad view, the big picture. There are many different kinds of surveys.

In an opinion survey, you collect opinions from a number of people in a group or neighborhood. What's the point? Because it's hard to say what's best for people without first finding out how *they* feel.

For example, maybe you think that the trees on a lot in your neighborhood should be cut down to make room for a playground. But when you survey your neighbors, they don't agree. You've learned that trying to go ahead with your project probably isn't a good idea.

Collecting people's opinions isn't the only way to conduct a survey. Some students at Jackson Elementary thought their neighborhood sidewalks should be repaired. They planned to ask the mayor of Salt Lake City for help. Since they didn't think the mayor would have time to come to see the sidewalks for himself, the students did a photographic survey. In other words, they took the sidewalks to the mayor! They showed the pictures to the mayor and his council. They gave short speeches. Together, their speeches and pictures were very convincing. The result? The sidewalks were repaired.

> "It's a very great thing to be able to think as you like."
> **Matthew Arnold**

Remember the Jackson kids who cleaned up the hazardous waste site? As part of their work on this problem, they surveyed their neighborhood, looking for wells. They thought they could ask health officials to take samples of the water from the wells to find out if it was contaminated.

What kinds of surveys could you conduct? Brainstorm ideas. For example: How do students at your school feel about the lunchroom, school rules, running for class offices? How do people in your neighborhood think garbage collection could be improved? How do they feel about recycling, beautification projects, and so on?

You'll learn that surveys do more than gather information. They help you build coalitions of support—people who agree with your ideas. They help you to identify your barriers to your plan—opinions that are different from yours. What you learn from surveys might even change your ideas.

Professionals sometimes conduct surveys to try to find out how people will vote in an election. These are called *polls*. Have your parents ever participated in a poll?

Courtesy Barbara Lewis

Jackson kids conduct a sidewalk survey to encourage improvements near their neighborhood.

"There are two sides to every question."
Protagoras

There are many different kinds of surveys. Here are three main types you could use. Which one you choose depends on what you're trying to do.

1. **Opinion surveys** collect opinions of a group. Check out the example on this page.

2. **Information surveys** collect information.

3. **Awareness surveys** are designed to make people aware of a problem or situation. You can help shape people's opinions with awareness surveys by giving them information they didn't have.

···➤

Sample Opinion Survey

Sixth grade students designed this opinion survey to find out what neighbors thought about improving the nearby river park. The kids surveyed 75 people who lived near the river. Here are their statements:

SA—strongly agree   A—agree   D—disagree   SD—strongly disagree

_____ 1. A playground should be built along the Jordan River Parkway.

_____ 2. Filtering ponds should be built along the Jordan River Parkway.

_____ 3. A second bridge should be built over the Jordan River.

_____ 4. There should be a treehouse built in the Jordan River park.

_____ 5. The Jordan River should be cleaned up more.

And here's how they put together their results:

	SA	A	D	SD	Undecided
1.	*13	21	22	12	7
	17%	28%	29%	16%	9%
2.	35	28	1	3	6
	48%	38%	1%	4%	8%
3.	17	26	13	7	8
	24%	37%	18%	10%	11%
4.	14	25	15	13	4
	20%	35%	21%	18%	6%
5.	58	10	1	2	4
	77%	13%	1%	2%	5%

* number of people who strongly agree with question #1.

What do these results tell you about what the neighbors think?

TIPS FOR SUCCESSFUL SURVEYS

Surveys can be done almost anywhere: in a school, a neighborhood, a scout troop, a shopping mall. For some places, you may need to get permission first.

Surveys can be done in almost any way: in person, by phone, by mail, or by email. You can even post a survey on a Web page. These methods all have their own advantages and disadvantages. If you have access to a phone, this can really save time. The catch? Some people don't like to answer questions on the phone. Letters are great, but they take time to write, copy, and mail. And there's no guarantee that people will answer them. Email is quick and easier for people to respond to, but not everybody has an email account. If you post your survey on the Internet, you have to hope that other Web surfers will come to you, and your response might be low. So if you really want to know what people think, the best way is often to get out and ask them.

1 If your survey will require you to travel away from home or school, get permission first. For surveys done on school time, or as part of a school project, you'll need to get permission slips signed by parents or teachers.

2 If you'll be traveling in a school group, check to see if there are any district policies you have to follow.

3 You can travel by walking, by bus, or by car. If you travel by car, make sure that every adult driver has liability insurance and a seat belt for each kid.

> **········▶ IMPORTANT ◀··········**
>
> **Never do a neighborhood survey alone. Always get a parent, teacher, or other adult to go with you.**

4 You'll also need one or more adult supervisors or chaperons. Teachers, troop leaders, and parents are some possibilities.

5 If you think your survey might make a difference to your neighborhood or city, try getting some media coverage. TV and newspaper reporters might be interested in coming along when you conduct your survey. This is great, because media coverage can take your project to a much larger group of people than you could ever reach yourself. Find out more about media coverage on pages 74–80.

6 If you're someone who likes to chat, your survey will probably take longer to conduct than you expect. So allow more time than you think you need.

7 If you're collecting information or opinions, be sure to organize your questions ahead of time. If possible, limit your questions to five or fewer.

Copy and use either of the survey forms on pages 185 and 186 to write your questions and record responses. The form on page 185 records one person's responses to many questions. The form on page 186 can be used to record many people's responses to fewer questions.

8 Some people you survey might challenge your questions and disagree with your solutions, if you share them. Keep calm and stay polite anyway. Never speak or act rudely.

9 Take plenty of paper (or survey forms) and extra pencils. In your enthusiasm, you're probably going to break a few leads. Who has time to run back to school or home to sharpen a pencil? And it's disruptive in the interview if you have to ask for a pen or pencil.

10 When you finish your survey, organize your findings in a chart, report, or visual. This is important. Otherwise, why did you do a survey?

You can copy and use the form on page 187 to tabulate your results and write comments about them. (What do you think they mean? Were you surprised by what you learned? Can you create a bar graph or pie chart to better show the information?)

11 Present your findings to an audience—other students, scout troops, your principal, clubs, community or parent groups. Present them to an agency connected with your problem. For example, when Jackson kids surveyed their school to find out whether children had played on a hazardous waste site, they sent their results to the health department.

Don't skip this step. There's no point in doing a survey if you don't use the opinions and information you collect.

Check It Out

The Gallup Organization
http://www.gallup.com/
Information on polling. Visitors to this site can take a Gallup survey online.

Survey Research Center
http://www.princeton.edu/~abelson/
This Princeton University site offers survey research news, information, and findings.

STUDENT CRUISING SURVEY

This survey was circulated through four high schools to seek information on how students felt about setting aside a place for students to go cruising.

1. Do you cruise the mall?

Yes _____ No _____

2. Why do you cruise?

3. If an area is made available, would you be willing to cruise somewhere else?

Yes _____ No _____

4. Would you be willing to pay an admission fee at a new site?

No _____ Yes _____; If yes, which would you choose?

Per use fee _____ (like $1.00 per person).
Flat membership fee _____ (like $10.00 per season).

5. Would you like any of the following services at a new site?

Music _____ Arcade _____ Concessions _____

Other (list)

6. Would you object to security being provided at this site?

Yes _____ No _____

(Prepared by Rob Osborne, Alex Wooten, Lisa Dobson, and Rikki Ashley—Future Problem Solving Team, West Iredell High School, Statesville, North Carolina. Advisor, Karen Charles.)

KIDS IN ACTION

Courtesy Karen Nicksich

Whittier Elementary First Grade

Whittier Elementary School

Salt Lake City, Utah. Did you ever wonder what happens to those plastic toys that fast-food restaurants sell to kids along with the burgers and tacos? Where do all the race cars, dinosaurs, alien life forms, and television characters go after the kids exit with their loot?

Kids in Whittier Elementary's first and second grades for gifted students wondered the same thing. How much money did restaurants spend to make toys that the kids didn't really want? They said to their teacher, Karen Nicksich, "Maybe that money is just a waste."

So the kids designed a survey for 600 children, ages five to 12, to find out what kids did with their toys. The results were no big surprise to them. Only 1 percent kept their toys from the fast-food chains. Most of the toys ended up squashed on backseats of cars, later to be chucked into the garbage with a residue of sugar toasties and broken crackers.

Kids didn't really want the toys, and the surveys showed they'd forgo the toy if the money the restaurants spent on them would be donated to a good cause.

The kids made bar graphs and pie charts to display their findings. And then they wrote letters to the managers of local fast-food chains, inviting them to their school to discuss the results of their survey.

"We think you should let kids choose how they want the money used," they told the managers of Taco Time. The restaurant listened when the kids suggested, "We could call the program 'Make the Choice at Taco Time,' and kids could mark a ticket or placemat to show how they wanted the money used."

The kids met to brainstorm an enormous list of causes the money could benefit. They finally carved it down to four choices for kids to donate the toy money to: families, animals, sick children, and the arts. Then they created placemats that Taco Time could use to advertise the program.

They proved that even first graders aren't too young to try to help others.

POWER PETITIONS

"No one listens to me!" How many times have you said that? It's a common complaint. But you can do something about it. You can collect other voices and create a louder noise—one that's harder for people to ignore.

A petition is a paper with signatures to prove that many people agree with your position. It's a demonstration of group strength. It can be a very powerful tool in gaining the attention you might need for your problem or project.

Jackson kids have written several petitions. They gathered signatures from residents around the barrel site asking for removal of the 50,000 barrels. They circulated a petition, which they presented to the faculty, to gain permission to wear shorts in school during the last sweaty months before summer. (You can see this petition on the next page.) They passed around another petition asking for a sixth grade dance, and

another to get permission to chew gum in school (this last one failed).

Jason Weaver, a seventh grade graduate from Jackson, passed a petition around his trailer court in an effort to get a caution light by his street. "You took your life in your hands every time you stuck your toe off the curb," he complained.

A group called Kids Against Pollution (KAP) in Newport, New York, has circulated a national petition advocating state and national constitutional amendments to guarantee citizens' right to clean water, air, and land (see pages 134–137).

There are many examples, and you can think of your own reasons for writing petitions. However, presenting your petition to the right group is just as important as collecting the signatures. You must ask yourself, "Which person or group would have the power to do something about my petition?"

NOTE: The kind of petition described in this section is not the same as a formal petition to make a change in the government or to pass a law. A formal petition has certain requirements. You can read more about formal petitions on pages 110–111.

Jackson kids petition to encourage cleanup of a hazardous waste site.

Courtesy Paul Barker, *Deseret News.*

Petition

We the students of Jackson Elementary School would like to be able to wear shorts to school. The reasons for wearing shorts are:

It is very hot and some days gets to 90° (on an average 80°).

There is no air-conditioning.

It's very uncomfortable for the teachers and the students. We feel that we would be more comfortable if we didn't have to worry about how hot we are. We will be able to reason with you on some rules such as: not on crummy days or cold days, not wearing short shorts or tank tops or real short tops.

We think that if the students don't play and goof off with them, they can wear them, but if not that they won't be able to wear them for the next two weeks.

NAME	GRADE	ROOM
April Chacon	6th	23 Graves
Jamie Atwood	6th	23 Graves
hochann Juo	6th	23 Graves
Josh Foy	6th	23 Graves
Pete Barton	6th	27-Thompson
aaron Iversen	6½	23 Graves
Jason Weaver	6th	27 Thompson

TIPS FOR SUCCESSFUL PETITIONS

Copy and use the petition form on page 188, or create a form of your own.

1 Most of the time, you'll want to use regular 8 1/2" by 11" paper to describe your problem and collect signatures. But this isn't essential. For example, if your problem is school restroom reform, you might make a stronger statement by collecting signatures on a roll of toilet paper.

2 Give your petition a title (for example, "Petition for Traffic Safety").

3 Identify your group.

4 Identify the official or agency that will receive your petition.

5 Write a statement describing the problem you want to resolve or the plan you're proposing. This should appear at the top of every petition page so that people can't say they didn't understand what they were signing.

6 Provide blank lines after your statement for people to write any or all of these:
    a. their signature
    b. their class, grade, or group
    c. their school or hometown
    d. their address and phone number

Some petitions might require addresses as proof that the signers own property in the area (for example, if you're petitioning to stop a bar from opening in a quiet neighborhood). Also, you might want to contact some of your signers again. Give people the choice of listing this information.

7 Number the signature lines for easy totaling.

8 Smile! The better you treat the people you meet, the more likely they'll sign your petition.

9 Some people you ask to sign your petition might disagree with you. Keep calm and stay polite anyway. Never speak or act rudely.

10 When you're through collecting signatures, photocopy all the pages of your petition. Keep the copy in a safe place. You may need proof of the signatures later, if your original petition is lost.

11 Present your petition to someone who has power to act on your ideas.

KIDS IN ACTION

Earth Angels gather signatures on one of their many petitions.

Earth Angels

St. Louis, Missouri. The Earth Angels are truly "earth shakers." The environmental protection club in St. Louis has accomplished amazing things. The kids work on many projects to help endangered species, protect the rainforests, and prevent global warming. The Earth Angels have won over 100 awards and citations for their activities, including a Missouri State Senate commendation, a U.S. Congressional tribute, a letter of commendation from First Lady Hillary Rodham Clinton, and a citation from President Bill Clinton commending them on their environmental achievements.

One of the Earth Angels's specialties is to wield powerful petitions. They know that individual kids don't have much of a voice, but by representing many voices on a petition they really pack a wallop.

The 7- to 12-year-old kids meet in neighborhood clubs with the director and founder of Earth Angels, Neil Andre—a man who knows how to ask good questions and who allows these inner-city kids to find their own answers.

When the Earth Angels learned about an annual winter slaughter of the bison near Yellowstone Park, the kids created a petition asking that the killing be stopped, or at least handled in a more humane way. The kids researched another cause and petitioned to free a dolphin from a poor facility. Neither of their petitions achieved their goals, but the kids were proud that they had tried to make a difference. They took a risk and stood up for what they felt was right.

You might think this doesn't sound like much power. But the kids learned a lot about problem solving. They created another petition to save their city's beloved Forest Park from additional development. "This is the only real park we have," Jason Harrison complained. When the development measure came up for a vote in a local election, the Earth Angels passed out 3,000 flyers asking citizens to vote against it. This time they succeeded. The plan to develop the park was smashed by 90 percent of the voters in the areas where the kids passed out their petitions and flyers.

Neil Andre said to his kids, who banged triumphantly on his door on the way to school, "Now you know David can beat Goliath sometimes."

Check It Out

Are you interested in finding out more about the Earth Angels? Check out their Web site:

Earth Angels
http://home.sprynet.com/sprynet/nandre/

They also have a "sister site" on America Online:
http://users.aol.com/Tambo/index.html

POWER PROPOSALS

Pretzels could be called "crackers without a plan." They double back, cross themselves out, and never arrive anywhere.

If you have a powerful idea, don't turn it into a pretzel. Get it out there, where other people can react to it and act on it. Make a plan. Write a proposal.

This is actually a lot simpler than it sounds. A proposal doesn't need signatures, like a petition. You can present it to any individual or group you want to influence. It gives your idea punch.

You might design proposals to start clubs, to change old school rules or add new ones, to set aside a special day to honor someone, to make an official aware of a problem, or anything else you choose. You'll find an example of a new club proposal on the next page.

PROPOSAL-WRITING TIPS

Copy and use the proposal form on page 189, or create a form of your own.

 Give your proposal a title.

 Name who you will present it to.

3 Identify your group.

4 Record the date.

 Write a brief description of what you hope to accomplish.

 Describe your plan of action, or how you'll carry out your idea.

7 Write a *needs statement*, which lists any equipment or services you'll need.

8 Make a budget. This might include fundraising plans. (Learn about fundraising on pages 65–71.)

9 Include a timeline showing when your project will begin and how long it will continue.

10 If possible, present your proposal in person.

11 If you plan to mail your proposal, write a short cover letter to go with it.

A PROPOSAL FOR A HIKING CLUB
PRESENTED TO THE FACULTY
AT NORTHWEST JUNIOR HIGH
September 20, 1997

We, the students of Room 115, want to organize a hiking club for the eighth grade. The club will meet on the last Friday of every month and will plan three hikes during the year. A bus will drive the students to the hiking area.

Plan

1. Miss Tolman will be the faculty sponsor.
2. A survey of the students proved there are many who are interested.
3. We could meet in Miss Tolman's room to plan the hikes.
4. Miss Tolman knows a professional climber who will train everyone.

Needs

1. Climbing equipment.
2. Bus to drive students to climbing areas and to return students to school.

Budget

1. One bus — at $150.00 rental (3 times) $450.00
2. Equipment per student (used) $75.00
3. The money will be raised at a white elephant sale to be held the second Friday of October after school.

Courtesy Erica Wright

Marieo Henry volunteers at Detroit's Westside Cultural and Athletic Club.

Marieo Henry

Detroit, Michigan. When Marieo Henry was 14 years old, his baseball coach was ambushed and shot in the head on his way home from Detroit's Westside Cultural & Athletic Club where he volunteered. "There were five to 10 violent deaths a year in the neighborhood," Marieo remembers. "I was sad because my coach had been my mentor."

Marieo helped his counselor at Earhard Middle School write a conflict resolution book, and the idea popped into his head that he might share all the research he'd done with the athletic club. Somebody had to teach the teens in the neighborhood how to cope with anger and resolve conflicts peacefully.

"I told the athletic club director, Erica Wright, about my idea," says Marieo. "She helped me write a proposal for a conflict resolution program. The program would help kids vent their emotions through discussion and mediation. We'd train teen mediators how to sit down with people and settle disputes."

The interesting thing about writing proposals is that people often pay attention. The club listened, liked the idea, and then named Marieo the director of the program. He trains kids from ages five through 16 in conflict resolution skills. The amount of violence among teenagers in the club has been dramatically reduced since the program began operating two years ago. It has helped thousands of kids.

"More organizations should do this to reduce violence and to offer help for kids who are violent," Marieo explains. "I think it's very rewarding to see the mediators' self-esteem go up. They become connected to the community and watch over it instead of leading to its decline."

POWER FUNDRAISING

Fundraising can be fun. And if you can put money where your mouth is—if you can solve your problem or support your project with dollars you donate—this can sometimes persuade officials to act on your ideas.

Fundraising can also be a good learning experience. Handling money gives you a hands-on chance to collect sizable sums and keep track of them. Just remember these two important tips:

- Save the money you collect in a safe place, such as a bank.
- Make sure that at least two people stay with the money at all times until it's deposited.

Kids have successfully raised money in many ways. Here are some suggestions for you to try.

FIVE WAYS TO FUNDRAISE

1 Sell something. Schools or groups can raise amazing amounts of money through sales. Try selling seemingly useless objects at a white elephant sale. Besides, parents will appreciate it if you and your friends strip your bedrooms of all the wheelless cars and abandoned Barbie dolls. It's a lot of work, but every dollar you bring in is pure profit.

You can also raise dough by pitching commercially prepared food: pizzas, popcorn, or candy bars. Food producers or businesses will sometimes donate these items, if you give them free advertising in return.

Would you rather sell homemade goodies? Check first to see if your state requires you to have a food handler's license.

Try your hand at other creative endeavors as well. You can make and sell cards, giftwrapping, buttons, and more.

2 Sell your services. If you'd rather hire out your time and energy, you can make money through your work. Offering lawn services, snow shoveling, local tours, car washes, and babysitting services can help you bring in the funds you need.

In some states, it's legal during elections to get paid to campaign for officials who are running for office. However, this activity should probably not be connected with a school, and probably should be supervised by parents.

3 Ask for donations or sponsorships. Businesses may donate time and materials to help you with your problem or project. Employees may be willing to work with you. Printers may agree to print letters or leaflets for free. Sometimes a local business may be willing to fund your project if you agree to identify it as a sponsor.

Your school or community may also give you money to raise money. For example, a service organization may pay your mailing costs for sending a fundraising letter. (You'll find an example of a fundraising letter on page 66.) You can post your letter on the Internet on your school's home page or send email directly to other schools, clubs, or organizations to ask for donations.

4 **Hold an event.** Dances, talent shows, concerts, auctions, carnivals, film showings—all these events and more can help you raise money for your cause. For inspiration from some kids who held a huge event, see page 73.

5 **Apply for a grant.** A grant is money given to a person or group for a specific purpose. Grants can help you get large sums of money, but they require planning and patience. Read more about grants on pages 67–71.

You can probably brainstorm many more creative ways to raise money. So go for it!

Salt Lake City School District

Jackson Elementary School
750 West 200 North
Salt Lake City, Utah 84116

To Whom It May Concern:

Thanks for your many pledges. Our bill has passed the legislature, and the governor has signed it. It is now a law. The law sets up a State Contributory Superfund to help clean up hazardous waste. It is now a legal fund.

We would like to thank you very much for your support. You may now send in your pledge in the amount of _____ to the following address:

Jackson Contributory Superfund
c/o Salt Lake Education Foundation
440 East First South
Salt Lake City, Utah 84111

Thank you again.

Sincerely,

Christina Lingbloom
Lauren Evans

Lauren Evans,
Christine Lingbloom, and

All Children in the
Extended Learning Program

··········▶ Check It Out ◀··········

Better Than a Lemonade Stand: Small Business Ideas for Kids by Daryl Bernstein, (Hillsboro, OR: Beyond Words Publishing, Inc., 1992). 15-year-old author describes dozens of money-making ventures, including curb address painter, birthday party planner, disc jockey, house checker, photographer, and sign maker.

Kid Cash: Creative Money-Making Ideas by Joe Lamancusa (New York: Tab Books, 1993). Creative suggestions for earning money, samples of advertising flyers, and tips on what to charge for your services and how to keep records. Written by a 14-year old with firsthand experience running his own business.

The Kids' Guide to Money: Earning It, Saving It, Spending It, Growing It, Sharing It by Steve Otfinoski (New York: Scholastic, 1996). How to earn money, save for a big purchase, understand the stock market, choose a worthy cause for charity, avoid getting ripped off, and more.

GRANTS: WHERE THE BIG MONEY IS

Another way to raise funds is by getting a grant. (A *grant* is a sum of money that is given to a person or group for a specific purpose.) To get a grant, you first have to know where to look. Government agencies, corporations, and foundations are all good sources of grant money. Second, you have to apply for grants. Making out applications can be complicated and time-consuming, but very worthwhile if you receive the money you request.

Even after you get a grant, your work may not be finished. Special grants called *matching grants* require you to "match" all or part of the grant with money you raise in other ways. For example, let's say your group applies for a $1,000 grant to make repairs in a neighborhood park. You win the grant—but to get it, you have to raise $300 on your own. (This would be a 30 percent match.) So you hold a white elephant sale at the park building.

If you're willing to make the effort to find and apply for grants, the rewards can be huge—hundreds, even thousands of dollars to fund your idea.

GOVERNMENT GRANTS

Jackson students have applied for many grants: to plant trees, spruce up the neighborhood, and fight crime. When the grants called for a match, the children peddled candy bars, popcorn, and pizza. The children also went to the state legislature to ask for money for kids all across Utah to plant trees in their neighborhoods. The legislature

liked the idea and has continued to fund this project each year.

Grant money is available through many federal and state agencies. It's worth going after, especially if you need large sums. You might be surprised at how much money is available, if you can find it.

Most states, cities, and towns also have grants available. You just have to get out your Sherlock Holmes magnifying glass and go snooping.

Officials aren't used to receiving requests for grant money from kids. For that reason, you'll probably get their attention more easily than an adult group.

Check It Out

The Catalogue of Federal Domestic Assistance (U.S. Government Printing Office, published annually). Describes federal programs and services that provide assistance or benefits to American people. Lists sources of federal grant money by agencies, tells how to apply, gives regulations, etc.

Federal Register is a weekly publication that lists announcements related to education funding and grantwriting. Available at libraries or on the Internet at *http://www.nara.gov/fedreg/*, where it also has links to numerous funding sites.

GrantsWeb
http://web.fie.com/cws/sra/resource.htm
Organizes links to grants-related Web sites and information, including government resources, private funding resources, policy and legislation information, and general grant resources.

Nonprofit Gateway
http://www.nonprofit.gov/
This site contains links for information on a variety of government grants.

GRANTS FROM CORPORATIONS

Kids Against Pollution (KAP) in Closter, New Jersey, needed help implementing a national information campaign. They received a grant of $85,000 worth of IBM computer equipment, sponsored by IBM and *U.S. News & World Report*. (To learn more about KAP, see pages 134–137.)

Many corporations can donate up to 10 percent of their taxable income to charitable organizations. That means *you*. And if you're asking, "How can I find out who the corporations are?" you've already taken the first step.

1. **Call your chamber of commerce.** Ask for a pamphlet listing the major corporations in your state. Many state chambers publish these.

2. **Call or visit your city library.** Ask at the reference desk where you can find a list of major corporations in your city or state.

3. **Call your mayor, city, or county offices.** They will often know about special grants you could get to help with a project. Special committees may have money, too—arts councils, city beautification committees, and so on.

4. **Call your school district offices.** They often have a person in charge of fundraising. This person can help you locate other sources to check.

It sounds crazy, but a great deal of money available to communities for improvements never gets used.

Check It Out

Look for these books at your library reference desk. They will tell you a lot about leading corporations. You could try contacting one or more. Ask if they would be willing to sponsor your group with a grant of money.

Million Dollar Directory: America's Leading Public and Private Companies (Dun & Bradstreet, 1997). A directory of 160,000 leading companies. Gives addresses, phone numbers, annual sales, contacts, etc.

Taft Corporate Giving Directory: Comprehensive Profiles of America's Major Corporate Foundations and Corporate Charitable Giving Programs (The Taft Group, 1997). Listed by subject. Examples: arts, civic and public affairs, education, health. Tells who to contact, plus how and when to apply. This easy-to-use book walks you through the process for each corporation.

GRANTS FROM FOUNDATIONS

A *foundation* is an institution that makes funds available for the public good. Some foundations get their money from private sources. You may have heard of some of these *private foundations:* the Ford Foundation, the Carnegie Foundation, the Rockefeller Foundation, the Lilly Endowment. All were started by very wealthy people who wanted to use their money to benefit society. In other words, the whole reason foundations exist is to give away money!

Community foundations are similar to private foundations, except their money comes from many public sources such as individuals, churches, and government agencies. Community foundations exist to benefit a specific geographical area.

As you find out more about foundation grants, you'll probably be amazed at how much money is out there, just waiting for someone to apply. To find out who's giving in your area, pick up the phone or head for your library.

1. **Contact your chamber of commerce.** Ask if it publishes directories of major clubs and associations in your state. Staff should at least be able to tell you which groups to contact, like the Kiwanis, Lions, or other service clubs. Some chambers have money of their own available for worthwhile projects.

2. **Check the Foundation Center's regional collections (in city libraries).** These resources might also have information on community sources of grant money.

The Foundation Center ◄ ·· ··············

The Foundation Center is an independent national service organization set up to provide information on foundations and corporate giving. The center provides many resources for locating grant sources and applying for grants.

The best place to start looking for grants is in printed directories or other materials available at Foundation Center regional library collections (most major city libraries function as regional collections.) You can find lists of foundations and the amounts of money they grant to different groups. Many of the regional collections publish an annual report. You don't even have to go there in person—you can usually call on the phone and request the information you need.

Look for these books at your library reference desk. (Sometimes this information is also available on CD-ROM):

- *A Foundation Directory* (The Foundation Center, current edition). Provides information about private and community foundations, their purposes, support, and limitations.

- *The Foundation Grants Index* (The Foundation Center, current edition). Lists grants by state. The Foundation Center also publishes volumes of grants according to subject—for example, family services, community and urban development, elementary and secondary education, science, recreation, etc. Ask about any rules they may have for people or groups who apply for grants.

- *Grant$ for Children and Youth* (The Foundation Center, current edition). Describes grants to nonprofit organizations in the U.S. and abroad for youth-related activities. Examples: service programs, education, health, medical care, programs for parents and teachers. Lists national foundations and how to contact them.

The Foundation Center Web site (*http://www.fdncenter.org/*) offers a database of corporations, private foundations, and community foundations that offer grants. You have two search options: (1) browse an alphabetical list to link directly with a particular grantmaking organization, or (2) search by subject or geographic keyword to zero in on a funding source. The site also offers a worksheet that you can use to keep track of information on funders who might be interested in your project.

You might ask yourself, "Why should I spend time doing research at the library if this is all online?" Well, you risk missing out on most of the money if you only look on the Web. According to the Foundation Center, there are nearly 39,000 foundations but fewer than 500 currently have Web sites!

HOW TO WRITE A WINNING GRANT APPLICATION

You've discovered a grant you want to apply for. Before you ask for a grant application, you need to find out if kids are eligible for that particular grant.

If your project is school-related, you may need district permission to apply for a grant. And you'll want to know if there are any restrictions on how you can spend the grant money, if you get it. For example, if what you want to do is repair your park, it doesn't make sense to apply for a grant that can only be used to buy library books.

Does the grant specify matching money? If it says that you must raise 20 cents for every dollar of grant money, can you do it?

How fast do you need the money? Federal grants usually require a six- to eight-month waiting period between the time they award a grant and the time they make the money available. If a federal grant is in your future, be sure to plan ahead.

And make sure that you've thoroughly researched your problem before applying for a grant. You'll need to explain your case clearly, positively, and in detail. Many more people and groups may be applying for the same grant. You must convince the granting organization that your project is the most worthy one.

When you're ready to apply for your grant, use the grant application checklist on page 190 to organize your information before you fill out the application.

▶ IMPORTANT ◀

Keep copies and records of EVERYTHING you do to apply for your grant and achieve your goals. Keep track of when and how you spend the grant money. The more records you have—and the more complete they are—the better.

KIDS IN ACTION

Courtesy Neil Andre

Earth Angels

St. Louis, Missouri. "Why don't we sell stock to raise money?" Anthony Huckleberry asked his Earth Angels club advisor, Neil Andre.

"Businesses sell stock. We get donations," Mr. Andre, founder of the environmental protection club, answered. But Anthony and the other seven-to 12-year-olds in the neighborhood club hounded the advisor until he relented. "Okay, we'll try it," Mr. Andre agreed.

The kids decided that anyone who paid a dollar would get one share of stock in Earth Angels. Stockholders would become lifetime members of the club and could vote through the newsletter on how to spend the club's funds. And the Earth Angels would have money to make a difference in the environment.

"One dollar for one share," the kids said. Adults in the neighborhood chuckled when they heard what the kids were trying. After the kids posted their stock offering on the Internet and were written up in many magazines, the idea grew. Now 30,000 shares later, no one is laughing.

The Earth Angels have used the money they raise to support their environmental work:

- Creating The Forest of Life in St. Louis's Forest Park, where each year they plant one large tree for each child who died by violence in the city the year before.
- Creating seven inner-city wildlife habitats certified by the National Wildlife Federation.
- Purchasing rainforest acreage to save the trees from being cut down.
- Purchasing solar cookers for rain forest villages to reduce the need for cutting trees for firewood.
- Protecting the Sandy Island Eagle Sanctuary and helping to clean up this important site.

▶ Check It Out ◀

Are you interested in finding out how the Earth Angels sold their stock or how to become a lifetime member of the Earth Angels? Contact them to find out more:

Earth Angels
8448 Evans Ave.
St. Louis, MO 63121
http://home.sprynet.com/sprynet/nandre

KIDS IN ACTION

Alex and Cameron Moore with baby Elisa, sitting on a quilt made by Treasure Mountain Middle School.

Courtesy Randy Olsen

Alex and Cameron Moore

Park City, Utah. When seventh-grader Alex Moore learned that the vice principal of his school, Treasure Mountain Middle School, had a 16-month-old daughter with leukemia, he wanted to help.

"I wonder how they can afford to pay for all this? Elisa needs lots of chemotherapy at the hospital. I wonder how we could help," Alex said. Then he got a big idea, "Maybe we could have an auction to raise money. The Boys and Girls Club did that." And his singing, dancing, and performing group, On Stage Studios, could perform for free.

Alex's younger brother, fifth-grader Cameron Moore, grew excited about the benefit. Two other friends, Christina Mason and Andrew Schaffer, joined in. "We could have a big dinner," Cameron said. Christina piped in, "And get people to pay for the dinner. And we could sell things there."

The kids went to work, but despite their efforts, not many people were buying the $25 tickets for the benefit dinner.

Then Cameron had an even *bigger* idea, "I'll bet if we got Mark Eaton to be the MC at the dinner, lots of people would come." Mark Eaton

played center for the Utah Jazz basketball team, and he lived in Park City, too.

Cameron warmed up his word processor to write a letter—he hated writing by hand—and faxed it to Mark Eaton. He didn't get an answer. Impatient, he bugged his mom, Tina Moore, to drive him to Mark Eaton's home.

When Cameron rang the doorbell, his heart was pounding. *A little girl needs my help,* he reminded himself. *A little girl with leukemia.*

When Mark came to the door, Cameron looked up, and up, and up, all seven feet six inches. Maybe his idea was a little too *big.* He froze and couldn't speak. But Mark encouraged him—and liked the idea. In fact, he liked it so much; he cancelled a radio interview to attend the benefit.

He showed the kids how to write a press release and call the local radio and TV stations to get their information out. The boys and Christina appeared in the announcements with big Mark Eaton, and donations began pouring in.

The boys personally contacted 80 sponsors. More than 200 people bought tickets to the benefit, and the kids raised $3,400 for baby Elisa. The money kept coming in. The kids beamed when they handed over the check to the vice principal.

POWER MEDIA COVERAGE
AND ADVERTISING

Wouldn't it be thrilling to see yourself in the newspaper or on TV? It could happen to you. And there's a way to make it happen: Plan an event, then put out the word!

Believe it or not, radio, TV, newspapers, and magazine reporters don't have crystal balls where they can see everything that's going on in a city. They rely on news tips from the public. That means you. And here's more good news: Reporters love to cover stories of kid action.

When reporters show up at your school or project site, hefting their heavy cameras and equipment, it adds an air of excitement and suspense. More than anyone, reporters can create public awareness of your project. You might receive some well-deserved pats on the back. And you'll attract more people who want to join your team.

Never apologize for seeking publicity, and never act embarrassed when reporters respond. That's their job. Reporters want good stories. If your project will benefit your community, everyone should know about it.

So let the media spread your message. Here are some tips to get you started.

ATTENTION-GETTING TIPS

1 Look up radio stations, TV stations, newspapers, and magazines in the yellow pages or on the Internet. Make a list of their addresses and phone numbers.

2 If you're going to contact media people on your own, there are two ways to do it. You can call them on the phone and hope they will talk to you. Or you can take a more professional approach and send out news releases. (A *news release,* or *press release,* is a written statement describing an event that is sent out to members of the media.)

If your project is school-related, an employee in the district office may be assigned to write news releases for you. This employee might be called a "public information specialist." Give him the information you collect, and keep him up-to-date on your project.

Reporters may be more interested in news releases written by kids than ones written by adults (even public information specialists).

⋯⋯▶ Check It Out ◀⋯⋯

Broadcasting/Cable Year Book (Broadcasting Publications, Inc., published annually). A directory of TV and radio stations, with addresses and phone numbers, by state and city.

Gale Directory of Publications and Broadcast Media (Gale Research, published annually). Lists newspapers, TV and radio stations, magazines, journals, and other publications in the U.S. by state.

MediaFinder
http://www.mediafinder.com/
This site offers a searchable directory of periodicals, magazines, newspapers, newletters, catalogs, and mailing lists. It's a great site for locating media people who are interested in your subject area.

The Standard Periodical Directory (Oxbridge Communications, published annually). Lists newspapers, TV and radio stations, magazines, journals, and other publications in the U.S. by state.

DAILY NEWS
MAN BITES CANINE
DOG DIDN'T KNOW WHAT BIT HIM *see pg2*

"When a dog bites a man, that is not news, because it happens so often. But if a man bites a dog, that is news."
John B. Bogart

HOW TO WRITE A NEWS RELEASE

1 Give media people plenty of advance notice of your event. They should receive your release at least two to three weeks ahead of time so they can put you on their calendars. Mail a copy of your release to each reporter on your list.

2 The top of your news release should give the name of the main contact person (that might be you), a telephone number where the reporter can call to find out more, and the date of the news release.

3 The body of your news release should answer these questions: *who, what, when, where,* and *why*—the five Ws. (On some news releases, the "why" part is included in a paragraph labeled "details.") Keep your statements brief, factual, and clear. Study the example on the next page.

4 Try to come up with a "hook"— something to snag reporters' attention without giving away your whole story. If it's appropriate, use a little humor. It will make your release more memorable.

5 If you're going to act professional by sending a news release, then your release should look professional, too. It's a good idea to type it or write it on a computer. Double-space, and keep it to one short page if at all possible. You can also write it by hand, as long as it's readable.

If you absolutely can't survive without two pages, type the word "more" at the bottom of the first page, and type "-30-" at the end of the release. ("-30-" is a code that means "the end.")

Copy and use the news release form on page 191 to organize your information before you prepare the final copy of your news release.

·········► Check It Out ◄·········

Getting Your Message Across: Media Tips
http://www.lightlink.com/nysccc/MediaTips.html
Created by the New York State Citizens' Coalition for Children, this site offers practical tips on writing news releases, feature stories, and letters to the editor, as well as guidance for being interviewed and creating public service announcements and promotional flyers.

KidNews
http://www.kidnews.com/
KidNews offers writing and news from kids around the world.

·········► IMPORTANT ◄·········

Inform adult supervisors (your principal, teacher, scout leader, parent) about the event you're planning.

Tell them that you're seeking media coverage.

NEWS RELEASE

FOR IMMEDIATE RELEASE

Contact: Judy Gilder, Teacher
Calvin Taylor Elementary School
(555) 623-9555

April 8, 1997

What: Calvin Taylor Elementary students will plant 76 oak trees on the hill next to the Children's Museum.

Who: Eighth-grade students in the school service class are spearheading the project.

When: April 25, 1997. The project will commence at 10:00 A.M. on April 25 with an opening ceremony in which the children will explain their project. Mayor Michelle Nielson is planning to deliver a short speech. The planting will continue until 3:00 P.M.

Where: The hill next to the Children's Museum at Eighth West and Citrus Drive.

Details: The children raised $2,100 to finance the project through applying for and receiving a city grant, through weekly popcorn sales, and through the donation of 17 trees by Green Thumb Nursery. The children have dubbed the oaks with such unique names as "JFK" and "Dog's Re-Leaf."

WHAT TO DO AFTER YOU SEND YOUR RELEASE—AND WHEN THE REPORTERS ARRIVE

1 **Make telephone contact.** Once you've sent your release, telephone media people a few days before your event to remind them.

2 **Practice.** Although reporters don't like "canned" answers, practice ahead of time how you might answer questions like: What is your project? Why do you want to do it? What have you learned? How did you become interested in it?

If you practice, you won't find your tongue getting caught between your teeth when you're interviewed.

3 **Practice relaxing, too.** It's natural to feel nervous about talking to reporters. And remember: It won't really matter if you stumble while you're talking. Anything filmed by TV camera crews is edited before it's aired, and newspapers don't print stutters and mumbles.

4 **Prepare a one-page outline describing your project**—what you've done, what you're planning to do. Make copies to give to each reporter. This simplified press kit will help to ensure that reporters tell your story like it is. (A *press kit* is a packet of information—background facts, photographs, and so on—that is prepared especially for reporters. Press kits are often given out before press conferences.)

5 **Provide enough space for reporters, photographers, and their equipment.** Reserve a place for them to stand or sit where they can see and hear what's going on.

6 **Write down the names of the reporters who cover your event.** When you plan another activity, call the same people on the phone and tell them about it. They will remember you.

7 **When your event is over, send thank-you notes to all the reporters who came.** This is polite—and the reporters will love it.

8 **What if reporters don't show up?** Even if they told you they wanted to? Remember that reporters must cover many events, planned and unplanned. If someone robs a bank at the same time, they'll probably zip over there instead. Hold your event anyway.

Paul Barker, *Deseret News*

MORE WAYS TO ADVERTISE

Jackson kids plant trees near their school, providing a photo opportunity for local reporters.

News releases are just the tip of the iceberg when it comes to getting attention. Read about these other ways to advertise your project or event, then brainstorm more of your own.

1 Community calendars. Many neighborhoods and cities maintain community calendars of coming events. If you advertise here, you'll reach an audience of officials, as well as the public. Community calendars are available in a variety of media, including local newspapers, postings at libraries and grocery stores, radio and cable television notices, and the activities section of a city's Web page.

Check deadlines for entries. Write a few concise statements (who, what, where, when, and why) and give the name and phone number of a contact person.

2 Newsletters. Clubs, churches, and other organizations often send out newsletters. Why not advertise in these?

3 Personal interviews and talk shows. Did you know that TV and radio stations often allow free time for public comments? Call or write your local stations to ask for time to discuss your project on the air.

Many cable TV stations set aside blocks of time for community access. Maybe you can have your own show! A group of kids called the Tree Musketeers in El Segundo, California, wrote their own television game show, "Tree Stumpers."

4 Press conferences. A *press conference* is a meeting all media people are invited to attend. It usually lasts about 30 minutes and includes a question-and-answer period for reporters.

You should not try this unless you have a really good reason—for example, an important dignitary who will be addressing a vital issue.

If you do have a really good reason, announce your press conference with a news release. For tips on writing a news release, see page 76.

5 **Flyers.** Flyers are a fairly simple way to tell a great many people about your event. To get them out, you can use the mail, fax, email, or muscle power (in other words, hand-delivery).

Your flyer should be one page or less and should answer (you guessed it) the usual questions: who, what, when, where, and why. Also include a statement which gives people a reason to attend. What's in it for them?

Make your flyer interesting to look at and to read. Include a strong statistic, an anecdote, or a few fascinating facts. Use large lettering for the headlines. If appropriate, illustrate your flyer. Humor will grab your readers' attention.

PSAs WITH PUNCH

A public service announcement (PSA) is a short statement that advertises a community event or expresses concern for a problem. Most radio and television stations also offer free air time for PSAs.

A PSA is more formal than a personal interview or a talk show. Community groups are usually allowed specific short time slots—10 seconds, 20 seconds, 30 seconds, 60 seconds, sometimes more—to get their message across, so you must plan carefully. (Thirty seconds is longer than you may think.) Since there is a lot of competition for these time slots, you must have a project that will affect a large audience.

To create a strong PSA, you'll probably need help from professionals—sound experts or camera people. Contact individual television and radio stations for guidelines on length, content, and eligibility.

Sometimes stations will help you write a PSA. Write and ask them.

HOW TO WRITE A PSA ·····························▶

Before you do anything else, contact your local television and radio stations to find out if they have any special rules for PSAs. For example, will your PSA have to be a certain length? Is there a deadline for getting your PSA to the station?

Copy and use the PSA form on page 192, or create a form of your own. Remember to answer the five Ws: who, what, when, where, and why. Check out the example on page 81.

1 Write the name and address of your group at the top.

2 Briefly describe your *target audience* (the people you want to reach with your message).

3 List the dates your PSA should *begin* and *end* running on the air.

4 List a contact person (you?) and a phone number (yours?) the station can call to get more information.

5 Briefly state your topic (what your PSA is about).

6 Write the text. Read it aloud to see how long your PSA will be and adjust your text as needed to fit the time slot. You could include two versions: a short one (maybe 10 seconds) and a longer one (maybe 30 seconds). This will give the station a choice.

7 Be sure to tell the station how many seconds your PSA will take.

8 Write "-end-" at the bottom. This means that the text of the PSA is finished.

PUBLIC SERVICE ANNOUNCEMENT

JACKSON ELEMENTARY SCHOOL
750 West Second South
Salt Lake City, Utah 84109

TARGET AUDIENCE: youth groups, adult advisors
BEGINNING DATE: Sept. 1, 1997   ENDING DATE: Oct. 1, 1997
CONTACT PERSON: Donald Seher PHONE: 555-2022

MONEY FOR KIDS TO PLANT TREES

<u>30 seconds</u>   Plant a tree today to save our future. Trees save more than money. They can save our environment.

<u>63 words</u>   Trees recycle water and prevent soil erosion. One tree in its average 50-year lifetime will provide $62,000 worth of air pollution control.
One tree.

Matching grants of money are available to school children throughout Utah to plant trees. For more information, call 467-HERB.

- end -

(Written by Donald Seher, sixth grade, Jackson Elementary)

KIDS IN ACTION

Courtesy Michelle Scott

KidsFACE

Members of KidsFACE record their PSAs urging people to protect the environment.

Nashville, Tennessee. On a sunny afternoon after school, 20 kids in grades five through eight met with their advisor, Michelle Scott. These members of KidsFACE (Kids For A Clean Environment) at St. Henry's Elementary School in Nashville, Tennessee, were trying to create PSAs to urge people to take care of the environment. But so far, their PSAs weren't very good. Their music lacked punch.

Then Ashley Craw had a brainstorm. "Since we're in Nashville," she said, "let's contact the Country Music Foundation to see if they will help us get a couple of songwriters. The stuff we're writing isn't that great. They could really help us."

To the kids' excitement, the Country Music Foundation didn't have trouble finding songwriters willing to help out. The Foundation hooked KidsFACE up with musicians Mary Bomar and Bob Ritter, who helped them put their words to music. Here are the lyrics from two of the PSAs they created:

Jill Bader:
*We have to be able to join
hands to save the earth.*

Meryl Large:
*Think about what is important to you:
The land, the water, and the animals, too.
Treat them kindly, with respect.
The hope to save them is not lost yet.
Maybe you will understand,
The earth is in your hands.*

They recorded their PSAs in Studio B at RCA Studios in Nashville, in the same studio that Elvis Presley had crooned from in his early years. The kids sang and swayed with the music that Mary and Bob added to their words.

Then they mailed out 200 copies of their PSAs to radio stations all over the country to be played during Earth Week 1996. Wal-Mart also played them in all of their stores.

But what made them most proud was performing the songs for their school. A fourth-grade girl, Michelle Ising, said enthusiastically, "I can't believe someone in my school made something that was on the radio. When can I make one?"

Check It Out

KidsFACE
PO Box 158254
Nashville, TN 37215
1-800-952-3223
(615) 333-9879

Melissa Poe, then nine years old, founded KidsFACE in 1989 as an after-school environmental club in Nashville. By 1997, her club had over 300,000 members worldwide. At 17, Melissa stepped down as its leader and turned that role over to two new CEOs (child executive officers): 15-year-olds Ashley Craw and Rachel Jones.

KidsFACE encourages youth to be active participants in improving the environment. Free membership for kids and teachers includes the membership guide *Our World, Our Future: A Kid's Guide to Kids for a Clean Environment* and a subscription to the bimonthly newsletter *KidsFACE Illustrated*.

If a KidsFACE club isn't available in your town, write to find out how to start your own chapter.

Audrey Chase "up a tree" at the beginning of her newscast.

Audrey Chase

Audrey Chase is a Jackson Elementary student who tackled another great project. She wrote and appeared in a four-minute Arbor Day TV news story about the importance of trees. Audrey was contacted by Dave Block, a reporter from one of the three major TV stations in Salt Lake City. She wrote the script while sitting in the TV station studio, legs swinging beneath a swivel chair. Dave Block helped her put her script in the correct form. Audrey chose the people to interview and narrated the story herself.

**KSL-TV NEWSCAST
WRITTEN BY AUDREY CHASE
Age 10, Jackson Elementary
Salt Lake City, Utah**

AUDREY'S TREES

Hi, my name is Audrey Chase. I'm here to tell you that trees are my buddies. Trees are beautiful, fun to climb, and give us shade to cool us off in summer.

They are also good for building tree houses. A tree can also be a home for animals, and some trees give us food to eat.

But trees are not just for fun. They also help the environment. Did you know that one tree in its 50-year average lifetime can contribute $62,000 worth of air pollution control?

Trees are important to me so we can save our environment and live a more healthy life.

(Audrey hops out of tree.)

One tree can recycle water, provide oxygen for us, and control soil erosion at a savings of almost $100,000 . . . and that's a lot of money!

In my class at school we started learning about the importance of trees. I realized that if we didn't have trees, we couldn't live. I started looking for places that I could plant trees. I didn't want any open spaces, unless it was for flying kites or playing ball.

This is my front yard. Here is the first tree I planted. It's a honey locust. Since then, I planted ten more near the Children's Museum. I named these two trees. This one is named after Dick Klason, a state forester . . . and a big help. This one is named Ted E. Bear Lewis . . . he is a member of the state house of representatives. He helped us to get money from the legislature for more trees.

This is my friend, Aaron Webster. He thinks trees are important, too.

Audrey interviews Aaron Webster.

(Audrey interviews the Schauguaards about why they care for trees.)

I think trees are so important I wrote a letter to President Bush asking him to set aside money so kids can plant trees across the nation.

(Audrey is interviewed live by TV Reporter at Warm Springs Park with classmates. They end by planting a tree together.)

Audrey interviews Thelma and Burt Schauguaard.

Photos courtesy Barbara Lewis

POWER PROCLAMATIONS

You probably think that mayors, governors, and other officials are the only ones who can write proclamations. Not true! You can write one, too. It's easy.

A proclamation is just a fancy way of making an announcement to the public. It can also be used to recognize someone who has made an important contribution of some kind. Proclamations are usually made by officials, but there are no punishments awaiting inventive kids who write one themselves. You might like to recognize someone who has helped your cause.

Mayors are usually willing to make proclamations on your behalf. For example, suppose you want to advertise an anti-drug campaign. You could kick it off by asking your mayor to proclaim a certain week as "Kick Out Drugs Week."

Councils or commissions might also write proclamations or resolutions in much the same way. When a governor writes one, it might be called a *declaration*. Since "proclamation," "resolution," and "declaration" are often general terms, any official can create one on official stationery.

In the past, mayors and commissions across the nation have written proclamations for many different kinds of causes, including:

- Environmental Awareness Month
- Bike to Work Week
- Kindness to Animals Week
- Youth of America Week
- Random Acts of Kindness Week
- Banned Book Week

What would you like to proclaim? Use your imagination!

PROCLAMATION TIPS

1 Copy and use the proclamation form on page 193 to make yours look official. To get an idea of what to say and how to say it, study the example on page 4.

2 Contact your mayor's office at least a month in advance to request the proclamation. The mayor's secretary can set up a time and place for you to meet. You should also send a letter stating exactly what you would like the mayor to write.

3 When you arrive (preferably at the mayor's office) for your appointment, the mayor will probably have your proclamation ready. Usually, a mayor will allow you to take a photograph with him or her signing the proclamation. This photo can be used for advertising your project, if you get the mayor's permission first.

KIDS IN ACTION

Hawthorne Elementary kids open a recycling center in Salt Lake City.

Hawthorne Elementary

Salt Lake City, Utah. "Wait! Don't toss out that newspaper! Save that aluminum can!" The fourth, fifth, and sixth graders at Hawthorne Elementary in Salt Lake City, Utah, are serious about recycling. If one of these energetic kids can corner you, he or she will wring a promise out of you to save all your toilet paper tubes and old clothes hangers in order to make a super marble shoot for their "Recycled Invention Fair." Or Eric, Ernie, or McKay will sidle up to sell you their triangular shaped earrings made out of old cans. Only $2.00 a pair. What a bargain!

But their teacher, Sheri Sohm, encouraged them to think bigger. So the kids carried their recy-

cling idea to the community, collecting 15,000 cans at their school and starting the Sugar House Recycling Center for Newspapers. And some of the children have even served on the mayor's recycling committee.

They call themselves KOPE—Kids Organized to Protect the Environment. They have planted a garden in their school yard, written and presented plays, organized their own Earth Day art fair, and written a newsletter. They have started KOPE groups in other schools and hosted two meetings with 15 other schools to encourage projects to celebrate Earth Week.

POWER POSITIONS: GAINING REPRESENTATION ON BOARDS AND COUNCILS

Every time your local school board has a meeting, it affects you. Board members might make decisions about what requirements are necessary for graduation, when you have vacations, what you must learn each year, whether to adopt a year-round school, whether to shorten or lengthen the school day, and many more issues that determine what school is like for you.

There are probably hundreds of committee meetings in your community every week. These committees are making decisions that touch your life, including what rules will govern education, recycling and environmental choices, traffic regulations, health standards, and almost anything else you can think of.

But *where are the kids?* Are you sitting on those boards and councils, helping to make those decisions, or are you just accepting whatever they decide? You may not realize it, but you do have a choice.

And how about governing councils for 4-H clubs, Boy Scouts and Girl Scouts, youth leagues and societies, and sports organizations? Have you ever wanted to add something to a program or change a rule? Well, you can.

Children at Hawthorne Elementary in Salt Lake City served on the mayor's recycling committee, making suggestions about recycling aluminum cans and paper.

Many students serve on PTA boards. Some schools have formed PTSAs (Parents, Teachers, Students Associations). If you choose to do this, you'll probably have to pay dues, because PTSAs usually require dues from all members.

Jackson kids attended their local community council several times before it dawned on Kory Hansen and April Chacon to ask why kids weren't represented there. They asked for and won permission to sit on the council in an advisory capacity. (To be in an *advisory capacity* means that you can't vote on decisions. But you can offer your opinions and advice.)

Ben Smilowitz of West Hartford, Connecticut, was not content with serving on a student advisory committee to his state board of education. This savvy 16-year-old has been lobbying in his state to create two student seats on the state board. Ten states and the District of Columbia currently have student members—and four of those states allow student members to vote.

Do you want to help make important decisions? It won't happen unless you ask for the right. If you're interested, here are some tips to try.

TIPS FOR GAINING REPRESENTATION

1 **Find the right agency or council.** What kinds of things are you interested in? Follow one of your interests. Call your chamber of commerce or city offices (the mayor, the city council) to ask if there are any committees serving on that subject.

For example:

If you're interested in . . .	*you might try . . .*
animals	the Humane Society
environmental issues	the Sierra Club national wildlife groups
health issues	state health agencies Red Cross

Most communities have neighborhood councils you could attend. While you're there, ask for more suggestions of groups you might join. Or try your board of education. Why not?

2 **Use your social action skills!** You could pass a petition, gaining other kids' signatures, to ask for representation on a particular board or council. (Read about petitions on pages 58–60.) Let newspaper and TV reporters know that you're seeking representation. Making the public aware of your idea increases your chances of being accepted. (Find out how to get media coverage on pages 74–81.) You might also write a proposal. (Learn how on pages 62–63.)

3 **Ask about becoming a student advisor.** It's often easier for you to sit on a board or council as a student advisor than to become a voting member. But you can have power to influence decisions as an advisor.

4 **Meetings might be boring to you.** They will be less boring if you assert yourself and *ask questions*. Ask the other members to repeat or explain anything you don't understand. If you get involved in the discussions, meetings will be much more exciting for you. And you never know—you may even teach the committee a thing or two about how to get things done faster. Kids seem to know how to cut through red tape.

5 **Don't allow yourself to be put down by anyone.** Most people will appreciate your ideas. And most will answer your questions respectfully and explain things to you. You have a right to know what's going on and to understand it.

6 **Always be polite.** Even if you sometimes get discouraged or angry, don't be rude. ....➤

"Only those who dare to fail greatly can ever achieve greatly."
Robert Kennedy

KIDS IN **ACTION**

Courtesy R.J. Studios, 1997

Luhui Whitebear

Otis, Oregon. Luhui Whitebear speaks up and speaks out for native youth on a statewide board. As the only female youth representative on the Oregon Native Youth Council, she lets the adult members know what she thinks is best for young Natives. She talks to them about problems youth have with gangs, alcohol and other drugs, education. "It is important for youth to be on governing boards because everybody needs to have a say in what happens, and adults have more power to *make* things happen," says Luhui.

Luhui also serves as president of the Oregon Native Youth New Voices student organization. She visits youth in correctional facilities and writes letters to encourage them to improve their lives. One man in jail wrote a letter to the Youth Council, saying, "We are all tribal members, not gang members."

"That was really neat," Luhui says of the letter, "because that is true for *all* people. I was brought up to respect people, and it makes me sad to see them hurt themselves or others. They should get involved in good activities and share their culture." So she helped to start the first Native Students Association at Taft High School. They elected Luhui as president.

Luhui also loves to write and is a member of WordCraft Circle of Native Writers and Story Tellers. She has read her poems at several conferences. Her poetry helps to carry a hopeful message and to preserve the Chumash, Pueblo, Commanche, and Huichol traditions and culture of her family. Here's one of Luhui's poems:

People of the earth,
Close your eyes, and listen
to the wind.
Our ways are not lost,
Only forgotten. . . .

POWER CAMPAIGNING

You may not want to be a leader yourself, but it's your responsibility to choose good leaders to follow. And believe it or not, kids can campaign for officials, and they can turn the tide in an election.

The next time an election rolls around, don't just sit back. Get involved! Study the candidates and their issues. Read newspaper reports and watch speeches on TV. Then pick a candidate and find out how you can help.

CAMPAIGNING TIPS

1 **Include your parents in your plans.**

2 **Call your candidate's campaign office.** You might have to get the number from directory assistance or call your candidate's political party offices listed in your phone book. Or call your neighborhood council to learn the location of campaign headquarters. Pick up the phone or walk in the door. Tell them you're ready and willing to volunteer.

3 **Get involved.** You might get involved in attending meetings, helping with voter registration, handing out flyers, speaking door-to-door, interviewing, surveying neighborhoods, creating and distributing signs and posters, soliciting support from various groups, making telephone calls, and so on. For every political campaign, there are a million different things to do. Use your social action skills to support a candidate you believe in!

Kory Hansen

Salt Lake City, Utah. Kory Hansen went to a meeting at his local community council intending to ask why there weren't any kids on the council. When he arrived, he discovered that the candidates who were running for re-election to the state legislature were there, too. So Kory (who "turns on" if you put him anywhere near a microphone) gave his speech to council members and candidates.

Kory met the candidates for state office and asked them, "Is there any way you could help us raise some money?" The Jackson kids had just won the President's Youth Environment Award, he explained. They had been invited to Washington, D.C., to receive the award in person. They needed more money to get there.

Senator Rex Black, who sponsored the kids' hazardous waste bill in the Utah senate, told Kory that he might be able to help. If the kids were willing to go door-to-door, campaigning for his re-election, the senator would pay them $300 from his campaign funds. (This is legal in Utah if certain requirements are followed.)

Representative Ted Lewis, another of the kids' sponsors, was also up for re-election. The kids wanted to see their two helpful friends kept in office.

Because it's important in Utah that schools don't support one candidate over another, the kids met in the classroom *after* school (not during school time) to organize the project. Their parents came to the meeting and later traveled with them to each house over about a 40-block area. No one was required to do the campaigning. It was strictly a volunteer project.

Kory divided up the campaign material with his friends Aaron, Jami, and April. Then the Jackson kids went door-to-door, armed with their most winning smiles. They spoke with residents and left information behind. The people they visited were intrigued with the young campaigners. The kids got blisters from tromping over hard cement for a whole day, but in the evening, they fell on the grass and giggled.

Although one of the political races was tight, both Senator Black and Representative Lewis were re-elected. The kids received their money and learned that even children can help elect officials of their choice.

POWER VOTER REGISTRATION

Did you know that a lot of adults are numb? They're numb from the everyday grind of filling out forms, balancing checkbooks, changing diapers, and changing tires. In the process, some have forgotten the principles our country was founded upon. Many don't think their votes count for anything. They don't even bother to register to vote.

In the U.S. the right to vote belongs to citizens of legal age (18 or older). To exercise that right, people must register in their local *municipalities*—cities, towns, counties, or villages. Imagine what could happen if kids attacked their communities in a campaign to shake adults out of the mothballs. Picture what a difference this might make in your neighborhood.

You have the enthusiasm and the energy. You can do it. Along the way, you'll probably become so enthusiastic about the right to vote that you'll never grow into a numb adult yourself.

KNOW THE RULES:
REQUIREMENTS FOR REGISTERING AND VOTING

To register to vote, a person:

1. must be a citizen of the United States,
2. must be at least 18 years old by the next election, and
3. must meet local residency requirements.

> "America is a land where a citizen will cross the ocean to fight for democracy and won't cross the street to vote in a national election."
> **Bill Vaughn**

Residency requirements can be complicated. Call your local voter registration office to get the exact requirements for your area. Try the blue pages in your phone book under "voter information" or "village offices." Or call the League of Women Voters; you'll find their local number in the white or yellow pages.

- A person does *not* have to live in a community for a certain length of time to vote in a federal (national) election—for president, for example, or for a member of congress. (But voters still have to register according to their state's rules and deadlines.)

- Some states *do* have rules for state or local elections. Some states require that a citizen must live within the city, county, or village for up to 30 days before an election in order to vote.

Voter registration deadlines also vary from state to state. In some states you must register to vote a certain number of days before the election. For example, in Arizona voters must register at least 50 days before the next election; in Virginia, 31. In other states, voters can register at the polls on the day of the election if they bring valid identification.

In most states, voters can register by mail or in person at specific sites such as election offices, libraries, and motor vehicle offices.

If you are a regular voter, you only need to register to vote once. As long as you keep voting, you'll stay in the registration system. You don't have to register again until you move. But if you register and don't vote, after a certain time your name may be dropped from the lists of registered voters, and you'll have to register again.

There are two types of elections:

(1) *primary elections*, where voters choose the candidates who will appear on the ballot; and

(2) *general elections*, where voters choose the candidates who will actually hold office.

Depending on your state, each election type might have its own registration requirements. For example, to vote in a primary election, a person might need to register as a member of a certain political party, or register several months before the election.

HOW YOU CAN HELP GET OUT THE VOTE

1 One way voters can register is by mail. Mail-in applications are sometimes available at banks, libraries, post offices, or public buildings. You might be able to get mail-in forms from your registration office to deliver door-to-door.

2 In some communities, you or your group adviser might be able to check out a registration book from your county (or village) clerk's office and carry it door-to-door. With a registration book, you can register voters on the spot.

Copy the voter registration form on page 194 for an easy-to-follow script you can use when going door-to-door. Fill out as much of the information as you can ahead of time (part 1, part 2c), then make several photocopies to bring along.

3 You may meet people who say they can't vote or can't register for any number of reasons—they'll be away from home on election day, they're ill, they're disabled, or they're elderly. Let them know that absentee ballots are available especially for them. The voter will probably have to call or write for a ballot.

············▶ IMPORTANT ◀············

NEVER go door-to-door alone for any reason. **ALWAYS** get a parent, teacher, or other adult to go with you.

Even if several kids go together in a group, you should **ASK AN ADULT TO ACCOMPANY YOU.**

---

4 For many people, English is a second language, and they don't speak English well enough to feel comfortable with registering or voting. Many jurisdictions have *bilingual ballots* available (ballots written in English and another language). See if your election office has some bilingual literature explaining registration and voting. Bring some along on your door-to-door campaign.

5 Kids might be allowed to participate in telephone voter registration campaigns. Check with your registration office or a political party. You might work with a candidate who is running for office or with a political party by calling to remind people to vote.

6 Use your other social action skills—and your imagination—to get the job done. Write a letter to the editor of your local newspaper reminding people to vote (see pages 29–36 for letter-writing tips). Pass out your own flyers door-to-door (see page 79). Write a PSA (see pages 80–82).

·········▶ Check It Out ◀·········

Kids Voting USA
398 South Mill Ave., Suite 304
Tempe, AZ 85281
(602) 921-3727
http://www.kidsvotingusa.org/
This nonprofit, nonpartisan organization makes it possible for kids to visit official polling sites on election days and cast their own ballots on the same issues and candidates the adults are voting for. Studies are showing that the program increases *adult* voter turnout. Find out if your state is a member.

Project Vote Smart
Center for National Independence in Politics
129 NW Fourth Street, Suite 204
Corvallis, OR 97330
(541) 754-2746
Fax: (541) 754-2747
comments@vote-smart.org
http://www.vote-smart.com/
This national nonpartisan organization tracks information on over 13,000 candidates and elected officials. Packed with information, the Web site includes links to government and political sites, popular issues, and information on voter registration. *The Vote Smart Web YellowPages*, a free printed directory of government and issues Web sites, and the *U.S. Government: Owner's Manual* are available free by calling 1-800-622-SMAR(T).

"Bad officials are elected by good citizens who don't vote."
George Jean Nathan

Courtesy Lauren Mullen

Jackson Elementary students campaining for voter registration door-to-door.

Jackson Elementary

Salt Lake City, Utah. Fifth-grade students in Lauren Mullen's class hit the pavement just before election day, carrying signs that said, "Vote for President." They hefted voter registration books under their arms as they conducted a door-to-door voter registration campaign. They knocked at doors in their voter district surrounding Jackson Elementary in Salt Lake City.

At one of the first homes, a gray-haired woman opened the door cautiously, only her eyes and nose peeking around the corner.

Sean Westlund spoke up when the door opened, "Are you registered to vote? It is important to vote, because one vote can make a difference."

"I have never voted a day in my life," the woman confided. A faded blue dress appeared from behind the door as she cracked the door open further to see the kids. But she took the mail-in voter registration form and promised the kids she would vote as long as she didn't have to walk to the voter booth. She rubbed her hip. They registered her on the spot.

Mrs. Mullen's class had been studying democracy and also wanted to make a contribution to the neighborhood. Since the 1996 presidential election was looming six weeks ahead, they decided to see if they could get more people out to vote. Even though the voter registration books were checked out to their teacher, the kids did the actual signing up with the residents at their doors.

Breaking into teams with adult supervisors, they canvassed the neighborhood, registering 40 people, many who had never registered before. Then they received an added bonus. They checked out their own households and registered 15 members of their own families.

"Voting is good for the country. My sister votes each year," Karolynn Dixon said. Thanks to Karolynn and her classmates, maybe they will all vote in the future.

POWER ORGANIZING:
INCORPORATING YOUR ORGANIZATION OR GROUP

How would you like to put *Inc.* for "Incorporated" after the name of your organization or group? Does that sound impossible or scary? In fact, it's neither. Amber Coffman, the young woman from Maryland who founded Happy Helpers for the Homeless, has incorporated (see page 50). So has Kids Against Pollution (see page 134). Youth groups around the nation are incorporating their clubs into small, nonprofit businesses.

Why would a group of kids get this fancy? Usually it's because they want to have special status as a *nonprofit organization*. Translated, this means that not only can you identify your group as a specific club, but you also won't have to pay taxes on your club earnings in most cases. And, once you incorporate, you can apply for tax-exempt status with the Internal Revenue Service (IRS). Then people who make donations to your group can get a tax deduction for their contributions. This means you should be able to raise money more easily. Incorporating can give you credibility. It can also make you eligible for government or foundation grants.

If your organization is growing, you might want to consider incorporating. For example, your club might finance a huge mailing to kids or groups all over the country. As a result, you have some ongoing expenses and you raise funds in a variety of ways. You might even have to pay someone a salary to help out. This is a case when incorporating makes sense.

Incorporating as a nonprofit organization is possible, but it isn't easy, so you'll need an adult advisor to help. (Incorporating usually requires someone over 18 to be in charge.) There are also fees to pay along the way, so be prepared. Here are the basic steps you'll need to follow.

Check It Out

How to Form a Nonprofit Corporation (4th edition) by Anthony Mancuso (Nolo Press, 1998).

A guide for anyone who wants to start a nonprofit organization. Step-by-step instructions for all 50 states, plus complete instructions for obtaining federal tax exemption.

HOW TO INCORPORATE

1 Contact your department of commerce or secretary of state (or comparable office) to find out how to file *articles of incorporation* with your state. Articles of incorporation are the documents that etablish your group's name and purpose. You'll have to decide on a name for your group, tell your "duration of operation" (how long you plan to have a club), state your purpose and activities, and so on. You may want to design your own *logo*—a special symbol that stands for your group.

2 Get a business license with your city or county where you'll be doing business. Contact the business licensing division. Tell them what you plan to do, and they'll direct you to the right department.

3 Contact the Internal Revenue Service (IRS) to obtain a federal I.D. (identification) number.

4 If you want to be classified as a tax-exempt nonprofit organization, you have to make a special request to the IRS. Then you won't have to pay taxes on donations your group receives. And people will be able to deduct what they pay to you on their taxes.

5 Your advisor can check your *State Code* for specific details. All main libraries have enormous volumes of your *State Code*, which outlines all the laws in your state. Ask your librarian to help you find the one that explains how to incorporate.

If this is the kind of challenge you thrive on, go for it!

Check It Out

Legal and Tax Answers for Nonprofit Organizations
http://www.exemptlaw.com
This site gives clear, basic information on the advantages of incorporating and general guidelines on starting a nonprofit corporation.

KIDS IN ACTION

Chris Morris at the food bank.

Courtesy Chris Morris

Chris Morris

St. Paul, Minnesota. When 14-year-old Chris Morris first organized his Eagle Scout project, he had to twist the arms of his friends to get them to help him collect food for the local food bank. They scampered door to door, leaving grocery bags at 2,000 homes. That first year they collected 4,000 pounds of food.

But Chris realized that one load of donated food wasn't a permanent solution to hunger. It wouldn't take long for his mountain of cans in the warehouse to disappear, leaving an empty cavern. So the next year, he did the same thing again. More than that, he started his own organization, Neighbors Helping Neighbors. This time he didn't have to twist any arms. The young volunteers, aged 12 and up, remembered the glow they felt when they delivered the food the year before.

"That second year, we doubled our area and covered 4,000 homes," Chris remembers. "This is our fifth year now, and we reach 20,000 houses. With 200 volunteers, we raised 40,000 pounds. We had to rent trucks to haul all of it."

Chris continues, "But then someone called the Better Business Bureau to check up on us and found out we were just a bunch of kids."

The BBB told Chris that the donated food had monetary value. The law in Minnesota says that if an organization receives over $8,000 in donations in one year, it must incorporate as a nonprofit. Incorporation helps prevent legal problems and helps people know what charitable organizations to trust to spend donations wisely. Chris's project began to get confusing.

Chris explains, "Neighbors Helping Neighbors had many different sponsors. It would be easier for them if we *did* incorporate so that their donations would be tax-deductible. I thought it would make us more credible, too, in getting other sponsors. Now that project members are over 18, we can legally incorporate and become a nonprofit—we don't have to have an adult do it for us.

"But I want to make sure that our main focus is to always involve young people. I want to get kids on the board to learn how to run a nonprofit business. There is something inside everyone that expresses itself through community service. It makes you feel good."

PARADING, PICKETING, AND PROTESTING:
WHEN ALL ELSE FAILS

> **"To sin by silence when they should protest makes cowards out of men."**
> **Abraham Lincoln**

Have you ever seen crowds of people on the TV news carrying banners or signs, marching down a street or around a public building? Those people are parading, picketing, or protesting. They've reached the end of their rope, and they think that the only way to get attention from public officials is to put on a display of disagreement.

Parading, picketing, and protesting aren't against the law. They're protected by the First Amendment of the United States Constitution—the amendment that provides for freedom of religion, speech, the press, and "the right of the people peaceably to assemble." Even kids can parade, picket, and protest, but only as a last resort. These actions are legal as long as they're controlled.

Before planning a "PPP," get permission from your local police department and city offices (mayor or commissioner). Find out about any permits you need or special regulations you have to follow.

There are many other ways to protest besides parading and picketing. To *boycott* means to refuse to buy or use certain goods or services. Some kids have boycotted fast-food places that use plastic packaging, to protest against the possible hazards to the environment.

Walkouts or *strikes* occur when people leave a meeting, organization, or workplace to show that they disapprove of conditions or rules. Many teachers' unions have held strikes. Teachers have left their classrooms and refused to return until certain changes were made to their contracts or working conditions.

Sit-ins, sit-downs, and *demonstrations* are other ways people protest. Protesting is sometimes called *civil disobedience,* because people refuse to follow the established rules.

The main goal of most social protest is to get another organization or group to *compromise*—to meet and settle on differences of opinion. People protest most often when the other side refuses to listen to their concerns.

Because protesting can create disruption in the community, it should never be attempted without serious thought ahead of time. Talk with your parents or other adult advisors before ever trying it.

In other words: Save it for a *really* serious issue.

KIDS IN ACTION

Courtesy Dawn Webb

Dawn Webb

Winston-Salem, North Carolina. "One day I saw an ad at the local library for helping out with a teen crisis line," Dawn Webb remembers. That's when her volunteer efforts began.

In college Dawn volunteered at Head Start and at the Respite Center of Winston-Salem, North Carolina, working with mentally and physically challenged children. She gained great love for children and wanted all children to have enough food, clothing, medical care, and other basic necessities. So she took an internship with the Children's Defense Fund (CDF) in Washington, D.C. At CDF Dawn worked for children's rights, eventually becoming a regional coordinator for the nation's first Stand For Children Day.

The plan was to coordinate adults and children in a march on Washington, D.C., to show support for children's rights. Dawn organized a group of adults and children from the Winston-Salem region, and together they rode a bus to the nation's capital.

On June 1, 1996, Dawn's delegation marched to the Lincoln Memorial, banners in their hands, along with over 200,000 other people. Their banners rippled with slogans such as "Stand For Children," and "No child should be left behind." The huge rally for children was reported across the country on TV and radio. People watched. They listened to the message.

Peaceful demonstrations can make the public aware of your cause. Dawn's efforts helped make people think about children's issues. "I think it's important to help other people," Dawn says. "Especially if you are blessed enough to be *able* to help yourself. Some people aren't able to do that, like kids. Kids can't vote, but adults can."

⋯⋯⋯▶ Check It Out ◀⋯⋯⋯

Stand for Children
1834 Connecticut Ave. NW
Washington, DC 20009
1-800-663-4032
Fax: (202) 234-0217
tellstand@stand.org
http://www.stand.org/
This national nonprofit organization encourages people to work to improve children's lives. Contact Stand for Children to find out how you can join or start a Children's Action Team or be involved in the annual event.

WORKING
WITH GOVERNMENT

LOCAL LAWS

There's a city ordinance in Salt Lake City that makes it illegal to steal a parking space from a car that's already waiting for it. You might have a similar law in your city or town.

If you don't, maybe you should. And maybe you're the one who can do something about it.

Kids doing something about *laws?* Isn't that crazy? Not at all. Local governments tackle such problems as zoning, demolition and replacement of housing, multiple uses of buildings, uses of the downtown area, health issues, public safety, and highway improvements, to name a few. Some of these affect you directly, some indirectly. If you have an idea that could improve the quality of life in your city, why not try to turn your idea into law?

Kids *can* bring about changes at the local level of government. You can do this by using one or more of the social action skills described in Part Two: Power Skills. Or you can use these skills to try pushing through an actual change in the law.

special research project and share the results with your class.

How can you find out what kind of local government you have? Here are some suggestions:

1 Check your local telephone directory for the government section (often the blue pages). Call your local government offices and ask how your city government is set up.

2 Visit your library reference desk and ask to see The *Municipal Year Book* (International City Management Association, printed annually). This book is a good source of general information about local government.

3 As long as you're at the library, ask if there are other books specifically about your local government.

4 Invite a local official to come to your class and tell you about the government.

LEARN ABOUT YOUR LOCAL GOVERNMENT

Before you try to change local laws, you should know how your local government works. For example, a city may be managed by a mayor and a council, a council and a manager, or a commission. Or it may be run by town meetings, where voters meet to set policies.

You may be learning about your local government in school. If not, maybe you could suggest this as a unit of study, or do a

HOW TO INITIATE OR CHANGE A LOCAL LAW

Kids can't actually *make* laws or ordinances. Only officials can do that. But kids can ask officials to *initiate* an ordinance—which means that they can have an idea for a law and get the ball rolling. Kids can have a powerful influence on all lawmakers.

You might be surprised at your ability to present problems to officials and convince them to see your side of an issue. (On the other hand, you might change *your* mind after seeing *their* side.)

> "The only man who can change his mind is a man that's got one."
> **Edward Noyes Westcott**

Initiating or changing a law is basically a problem-solving process. This process is described in "Ten Tips for Taking Social Action" on pages 12–13. You may want to review those tips before you begin.

Suppose you pick a problem and research it carefully. You've looked at many possible solutions, but you think the best idea is to create a new law. You gather your evidence—facts, figures, photos, and so on—to make your case. A petition with many signatures can be very powerful (see pages 58–61) and can help you identify your supporters.

You should also identify people who might be opposed to your plan. Try to see their side of the issue and include their view in working out your solution. You might find that when working together, a new law isn't necessary. Or you may be all the more convinced that it's the right thing to do.

After doing your legwork, let's say you choose to go ahead with your solution and try to pass a new local law.

What's next? Here's a brief description of each step and where you come in in getting a local law or ordinance.

1 Contact someone who can help you. When you're ready, contact your local government (mayor, council, commission, administrator, or staff person). You can do this by:

a. telephoning (see pages 25–27)

b. writing a letter to send by mail, fax, or email (see pages 32–36)

c. making personal contact; for example, arranging for a face-to-face meeting or interview (see pages 44–45)

d. testifying at a meeting (see pages 120–121)

If your problem involves a specific location, invite officials to go there with you. Jackson kids met their mayor at a park to show him a bare hillside where the soil was eroding because there was no vegetation.

2 Discussion. Your proposed law will be discussed by your local lawmaking body. Meanwhile, you should be busy building coalitions of support among people in the community and schools. You should also continue trying to work with your opposition.

3 Investigation. Staff will probably study your issue to decide if there is a need for your proposed law. They may want to talk to both you and your opposition.

4 Legal review. Your proposed law will be investigated to make sure that it doesn't conflict with existing laws.

5 Drafting of your ordinance or regulation. Your proposed law will be officially written in draft (temporary) form, in legal language.

6 Public discussion or hearing. Your proposed law may be presented in a public meeting for other people to hear about and comment on. Call ahead to get on the hearing agenda. *Be sure to be there so you can testify in person.* (For testifying tips, see pages 119–120.)

7 **Signing, not signing, or vetoing.**
Your city's chief executive—your mayor, commissioner, or administrator—will do one of three things:

    a. sign your proposed law, making it a real law

    b. leave it unsigned, or

    c. veto it (reject it).

If the executive leaves your proposed law unsigned, it may become a real law anyway after a certain number of days. This depends on your local government.

Does your issue directly affect your local community? Exercise your rights as a citizen and try to instigate laws on noise pollution, graffiti, parking, curfews, youth representation on councils, speed limits in school zones—anything that would make your community a better place to live.

·············▶ Check It Out ◀·············

Local Governments by Barbara Silberdick Feinberg (Franklin Watts, 1993). Surveys the organization and activities of local governments across the U.S. Ages 9-12.

National Association of Counties
440 First Street,NW
Washington, DC 20001
(202) 393-6226
http://www.naco.org
This national organization represents county governments and helps them coordinate their policies and programs with each other and with other levels of government.

National League of Cities
1301 Pennsylvania Ave., NW
Washington, DC 20004
(202) 626-3000
http://www.cais.com/nlc/
This local government organization highlights resources for local officials and people interested in public policy.

U.S. Conference of Mayors
1620 I Street, NW
Washington, DC 20006
(202) 293-7330
http://www.usmayors.org/uscm/
This nonpartisan organization links the mayors of cities across the U.S. and helps citizens find out what's going on at home and across the country.

STATE LAWS

Creating a law to lower the speed limit in your neighborhood is one thing. But can kids initiate or change *state* laws? You bet they can. *You* can.

Kids all over the country have suggested and pushed laws through their state legislatures. Other kids have supported or opposed legislation in progress. It isn't as hard as you might think.

There's a national trend toward giving state legislatures more power. States now have more clout in deciding how to spend money they get from the federal government. As a result, state legislators are working harder to serve their *constituents* (that's you and everyone else living in your district). It's a great time for you to get involved.

LEARN ABOUT YOUR STATE GOVERNMENT

Before you try to initiate or change a state law, you should learn as much as you can about your state government. You will feel more comfortable and confident dealing with officials and lawmakers. And they will be more likely to take you seriously.

Maybe you're already learning about your state government in school. If not, don't let this stop you. Learn on your own.

State government, like the federal government, has three branches:

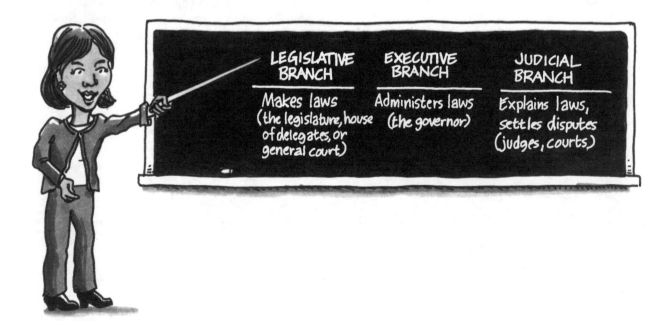

LEGISLATIVE BRANCH
Makes laws (the legislature, house of delegates, or general court)

EXECUTIVE BRANCH
Administers laws (the governor)

JUDICIAL BRANCH
Explains laws, settles disputes (judges, courts)

HOW TO INITIATE OR CHANGE A STATE LAW

Suppose you have discovered a problem and researched it. You've decided to try to pass a new law, or to change or oppose an existing law. (Take another look at "Ten Tips for Taking Social Action" on pages 12–13.)

You can begin to make or change a state law by contacting someone who can help you by introducing a bill. (A law you want to pass is called a *bill* until it becomes a law.) Or, depending on which state you live in, you can start a process called *initiative and referendum.* Here's a brief description of each way:

1 Contact someone who can help you. Even though you might write down your idea for a bill, it will still have to be rewritten in legal language. You can contact one of these people to help you put your bill in the proper form:

a. *Your legislator.* Legislators (state senators and representatives) are the people who make the laws in your state. Since you'll eventually need a legislator to sponsor your bill, this is a good place to start.

A legislator who represents your district is usually the best person to approach. Find out who your legislators are by calling your state capitol and asking. For a list of state legislatures and phone numbers, see pages 149–150.

Or you could contact a legislator who serves on a committee that studies your issue. To be polite, you should tell your district legislators if this is what you plan to do.

···▶

b. *Your governor.* While a governor doesn't make laws, he or she can suggest laws. And governors usually have a lot of clout with lawmakers. Be aware that governors are often too busy to handle requests. But if your governor happens to be a personal friend of yours, start here. Your governor can also tell you who on his or her staff could help you.

c. *A legislative staff person.* Staff people are the workers and researchers at your state legislature. One of them could help you get started. Staff people may be able to help you find a legislator to sponsor your bill.

Working with legislators to support or oppose a bill is called *lobbying.* See pages 113–121 for help with this process.

2 **Start the initiative and referendum process.** Some states share lawmaking power with the people through initiative and referendum.

Let's say that a group of people decide they want to make a new law or change in an existing law. Or they oppose a bill passed by the legislature and want to challenge it before the law takes effect.

To do this, they collect a required number of signatures on a petition. This petition is called an *initiative.* (This *formal* petition process is different from the *informal* one described on pages 58–60.)

Next, the petition goes either to the legislature for consideration or to the people for a direct vote. This popular vote is called a *referendum.*

What's your part in this process? Here are two ideas:

a. Contact your governor's office to find out if your state has initiative and referendum. If it does, find out the rules for your state. (Each state has its own specific rules for initiative and referendum.) Or go to the library and study your *State Code.*

If your state doesn't have initiative and referendum, you might ask, "Why not?"

b. Carry your petition to the voters and gather signatures. Kids can't sign formal petitions. Only residents who are registered voters can. But unless your state has an age requirement for circulating a petition, there's nothing to stop you from carrying yours to the voters. You would definitely need adult help with this, however.

What happens if your petition gets the required number of signatures? That depends on your state's laws. In some states, the proposed law or change goes directly to a vote of the people. In other states, it goes first to the legislature, so lawmakers have time to change or oppose it before people vote on it.

In either case, for your petition to become a law, a majority of the voters must vote for it.

Initiative and referendum

The following states and jurisdictions offer voters initiative and referendum:

Alaska	North Dakota
Arizona	Ohio
Arkansas	Oklahoma
California	Oregon
Colorado	South Dakota
Idaho	Utah
Maine	Washington
Massachusetts	Wyoming
Michigan	District of Columbia
Missouri	(Washington, DC)
Montana	Guam
Nebraska	North Mariana Islands
Nevada	

In addition, voters in those 24 states and jurisdictions—as well as voters in Kentucky, Maryland, New Mexico and Puerto Rico—can challenge a bill that has already been passed by their legislature.

How a Bill Becomes a Law

1. The bill is prepared

2. Introduced in one house in the legislature (your legislature may have only one house)

3. Reviewed by the rules committee

4. Examined by a standing committee

5. Presented at a public hearing (here's where you can have input)

6. Debated on the floor

7. The bill is voted on. If it passes, the bill is...

8. Sent to the other house in the legislature (unless your legislature has only one house)

9. Examined by a standing committee

10. Presented at a public hearing (here's where you can have input)

11. Debated on the other floor

12. The bill is voted on. If it passes, the bill is...

13. Sent to Governor. The Governor can sign the bill or veto it. If it's signed...

14. THE BILL IS NOW LAW

Jackson kids learn how to pass laws at the Utah State Capitol. At left is Representative Ted Lewis

Courtesy Gary McKellar, *Deseret News*

AMENDING YOUR STATE CONSTITUTION

Have you read your state constitution lately? If you haven't, maybe you should. You just might think of a way to improve it.

A change to a constitution (either state or federal) is called an *amendment*. If you've identified a problem, done your research, and decided that the best solution is an amendment to your state constitution, here's some information to get you started.

One important point: Constitutions are written to make amendments very difficult. Amending your constitution is an extremely long process, and you'll need lots of people on your team.

There are four basic ways a constitutional amendment can be proposed:

1 The state legislature may propose an amendment and submit it to the people for a vote.

2 In the following 17 states, the people may suggest an amendment by petition (initiative) and vote on it in a state election (referendum):

Arizona	Montana
Arkansas	Nebraska
California	Nevada
Colorado	North Dakota
Florida	Ohio
Illinois	Oklahoma
Massachusetts	Oregon
Michigan	South Dakota
Missouri	

If you live in one of these states, you could play an important role in passing a constitutional amendment. You would need to contact a government official (governor, legislator, or staff person), just as you would if you wanted to initiate or change a state law.

3 In some states, constitutional conventions may adopt amendments, if the people vote to ratify them.

4 A constitutional commission may propose an amendment. The legislature must then approve the amendment before the people vote on it.

LOBBYING: THE ART OF PERSUASION

> **"A president only tells congress what they should do. Lobbyists tell 'em what they will do."**
> **Will Rogers**

How can you convince lawmakers to support your bill? By *lobbying* them—the really fun part of the process. Lobbying lets you roll up your sleeves and try out all of your social action skills.

A *lobbyist* is someone who tries to convince a lawmaker to support or oppose a particular idea. In some states, lobbyists are professionals who are paid for their work. They must officially register with the state. In other states, anyone can lobby by picking up the phone or showing up at the state capitol and chewing the fat with her senator.

The word *lobbyist* comes from the practice of hanging around in the capitol lobby trying to get lawmakers' votes. Much lobbying still occurs outside the senate and house chambers.

As a lobbyist, you can have a lot of power, even if you're "just a kid." That's because you won't always be a kid. Someday you'll be a voter. Lawmakers realize this, and most of them also feel the need to represent the views of all of their constituents, including you.

Should you try lobbying? Only if you have a real problem and a real solution to present. Lawmakers are under a lot of pressure to consider all the *legislation* (laws) and *appropriations* (ways tax money will be spent) that come before them during each legislative session. During session their time is too valuable for you to tie it up simply for a learning experience.

Let's assume that you *do* have a good idea. Here are some tips to get you started as a lobbyist.

TIPS FOR SUCCESSFUL LOBBYING

1 **Research your issue well.** Know what you're talking about—whether it's an issue you're introducing, or one someone else has introduced and you want to support (or oppose).

2 **Start lobbying early.** Begin advocating your cause well before the legislative session begins. Much legislation gets *tabled* (set aside) because time runs out before it can be considered.

If you begin early enough, present your issue to an *interim committee*—a committee that meets between sessions. This will give you a head start on getting attention for your problem.

Interim committees often meet on weekends or three or four days a month throughout the year. Much legislation is shaped in these committees. You can appear at these meetings to speak about your cause or to get help from members.

Some state legislatures hold session year round, and some meet only every two years. Learn how your state legislature operates.

3 **Find a sponsor.** Look for a legislator who will support your cause and help you through the process.

If possible, choose a legislator from your district, one who believes in your cause and wants to help. She will have experts on her staff to research your project at no cost to you. Her staff will rewrite your ideas in legal language and proper bill format. Your sponsor will also introduce your bill to other legislators and speak in favor of it.

4 **Build coalitions of support.** Find others who are concerned about your issue (other schools? agencies? nonprofit organizations? youth groups? parents?). Organize them. Let them know what you're planning to do. Ask them to help.

5 **Try to work with your opposition.** Find out who or what might throw tacks in your path. For example, if you're trying to put through a clean air bill, industries that pollute the air might not be in favor of correcting the problem, since it costs money to modify or replace polluting smokestacks. Don't ignore them. Meet with them to hear their side of the issue. Include their point of view in your bill, if possible. Try to find ways to overcome their objections.

Identifying your opposition also saves valuable time. Lawmakers will want to know how other people feel before considering your idea.

6 **Ask for more than you think you might get.** Then be willing to compromise. Very little legislation passes exactly as it was proposed. Lawmakers may attach amendments to bills, or change bills into amendments to other bills.

7 **Acquaint yourself with the rules committee.** Each legislative house has one, which acts as the "gatekeeper" for legislation. The rules committee weeds out weak bills and decides which *standing committee* will investigate bills.

Standing committees (also called *permanent committees*) are the workhorses of the legislature. They cover areas like education, natural resources, health, social services, transportation, business and labor rules, and so on. You can usually go before these committees to speak for your cause.

As the legislative session nears the end, the rules committee can bypass standing committees to save bills from being tabled.

8 **Acquaint yourself with the appropriations process.** This is important if you want to have a say in how state money is spent.

The *appropriations committee* decides how the budget pie is sliced after the governor makes recommendations. It is usually made up of lawmakers from both houses. Your state may have several appropriations committees to study needs in major areas—the courts, business, labor, energy, education, and so on. A senior appropriations committee prepares a final budget act for approval by lawmakers.

9 **Prepare posters to bring to committee meetings.** (Check first to see if posters are allowed. Sometimes they aren't.) Your poster should present, reinforce, and clarify your idea in a visual way.

a. Make the words large enough so the whole committee can read your poster from a distance.

b. Vary the print sizes. Your main heading should be the largest.

c. Use color for more impact.

d. Try to stick to *one* main idea per poster. If you have several ideas to present, make several posters.

e. During the committee meetings, don't forget to use your poster. Point to it. Explain it. Repeat the idea presented on it.

10 **Prepare a one-page flyer to hand to lawmakers and staff members.** Your flyer should include:

a. your bill number, title, and content (what the bill says)

b. your sponsor's name and title

c. your name, or the name of the group you are representing

d. your reasons for supporting (or opposing) the bill

> "Everyone else is represented in Washington by a rich and powerful lobby, it seems. But there is no lobby for the people."
> **Shirley Chisholm**

Jackson students testify in the Utah legislature's house standing committee in support of the Hazardous Waste Superfund. Representative Ted Lewis is at left.

Courtesy Dan Miller, *Salt Lake Tribune*

e. your solution (which may be the bill itself)

f. your request for support (or, if you are opposing the bill, your request that the legislator join you in opposing it)

Make your flyer interesting to look at. Vary the size of your words, use color, add humor if appropriate. Legislators get a lot of flyers supporting or opposing bills. You want yours to stand out from the crowd. Making flyers by hand or coloring them could help your cause get noticed.

If it's absolutely necessary, you could add *supporting material* (more pages). But legislators don't have much time to read large packets of information. One page is more likely to get their attention.

Page 117 is an example of a flyer the Jackson kids prepared in support of their Hazardous Waste Superfund.

11 **Send thank-you notes to the people who help you.** This includes not only your sponsor, but also committee members, and other legislators you lobby who agree to support your cause.

12 **Remember that good public relations is essential every step of the way.** Never speak discourteously, even if your contact is rude. Never argue or threaten. A polite attitude might pave the way for a future success, even with your opposition.

Above all, be yourself. Be a kid!

H B. 199 State Contributory Superfund

for voluntary contributions

TO HELP CLEAN UP HAZARDOUS WASTE IN UTAH

Sponsored by: Ted Lewis   Co-sponsored by: Olene Walker

It will cost the state NOTHING.
It will benefit everyone

Initiated in behalf of Jackson Elementary students in the Extended Learning Program

UTAH SCENE

1. Utah has no superfund to clean up hazardous waste.
2. There are approximately 152 sites on the CERCLA list to be investigated as potentially hazardous places in Utah.
3. A 1987 report out of Washington D.C. ranked Utah 45th in the nation in developing environmental programs, including handling of hazardous waste.

DANGERS OF HAZARDOUS WASTE

1. It can cause birth defects, brain damage, neurological disorders, and many other kinds of diseases.
2. It can leak down and contaminate ground water, and then we drink it.
3. It can contaminate the air we breathe by being blown by the wind.
4. It can also contaminate the soils. Animals can eat food grown on contaminated soils. Then the chemicals can enter the food chain.

WHAT JACKSON KIDS HAVE DONE ALREADY

1. We held a Christmas Shop and White Elephant Sale and raised $486.22 which we would like to contribute to the fund.
2. At the beginning of January we mailed out about 550 letters to industries, environmental groups, businesses, and service organizations asking them if they would like to send pledges to contribute to this State Contributory fund IF IT IS PASSED. We have received over $2,192.00 in pledges thus far, for a total of $2,678.22.

PLEASE SUPPORT OUR BILL

LOBBYING IN PERSON

1 **Get permission from your sponsor and set up a time to lobby.** Find out from your sponsor if there are any rules for lobbying. For example, do you have to register? Do you have to stay in certain areas of the building?

2 **Be prepared.** Copy and fill out the form on page 195 for lobbying in person. This will help you to organize your thoughts. Make copies of the form to take along. Bring copies of your flyer, too.

3 **Prepare a short speech** (no more than three minutes). Give your speech to each lawmaker you plan to lobby. (See pages 48–49 for tips).

4 **Dress and behave conservatively**. Even though you might feel more comfortable in your favorite stretched-out tee shirt that says, "Nuke it all and start over," don't wear it to your state capitol.

5 **Arrive on time, but don't expect the legislators to be on time.** They may be voting on other measures, or they may be involved in a crisis or a long debate. Wait patiently.

6 **Ask each legislator you lobby, "May I have your support?"** This question requires an answer or commitment from the legislator. Make a note of his response on your lobbying-in-person form. If the answer is "no" or "maybe," stay calm. Don't act upset, disappointed, or angry. Above all, don't argue. Allow the legislator to express his opinion. You can lobby him again later by phone or letter.

7 **Tell the legislator if you are from his district.** Your cause is stronger if you are a constituent.

8 **Send them thank-you notes.** Don't forget people who help you—your sponsor, and anyone else who helps to set up your lobbying experience.

> **"You cannot shake hands with a clenched fist."**
> Indira Gandhi

LOBBYING BY TELEPHONE

If you can't make it all the way to the state capitol to lobby in person, you can still lobby by telephone.

1 **Get a list of lawmakers' telephone numbers, at both their home and state offices.** Your sponsor can probably get this list for you, or you can check for your state legislature's phone number on page 149–150 and ask for a list. During a legislative session, lawmakers try to make themselves easy to reach.

2 **Copy and fill out the form on page 196 for lobbying by phone.** This will help you to organize your thoughts and be prepared. Make copies of the form to use when you call.

3 **The best time to call is just before the bill is placed on the agenda for voting.** Your sponsor can let you know when this will be.

4 **Call during the day.** Many legislators might travel to their home district at night, and they may be harder to reach.

5 **Ask each legislator you call, "May I have your support?"** Note her response on your form. If the answer is "no" or "maybe," plan to lobby that legislator again in person or by mail.

6 **If the lawmaker isn't there when you call, leave a message and a phone number where she can return your call.**

7 **Keep a list of how each lawmaker plans to vote.** This will give you a good idea of how strong your case is—and which legislators you should keep lobbying.

LOBBYING BY TESTIFYING

To *testify* means to go before a group or committee and speak in support of your cause. It's a great way to lobby because you can reach several people at once.

Be aware that your issue will be openly debated. Legislators will discuss both sides, and your opposition will probably testify, too. It's a good idea to know what your opposition might say so you can try to answer their concerns.

Before the lawmakers are in session, you might be able to speak before interim committee meetings. Don't forget this important step.

After your bill has been assigned to a standing committee, you could appear to testify at the public meeting, if one is scheduled. Tell your sponsor so that you can get whatever permission might be necessary.

Testifying before the chambers of the legislature when it is in session is not often permitted because of time limitations. Check with your sponsor. Jackson kids testified on the floor of the Utah senate twice. Anything is possible!

Wherever you testify, here are some helpful tips to keep in mind:

1 **Contact your sponsor and get permission to testify.** Set up an appointed time. Find out if there are any rules you have to follow. For example, are posters allowed? How much time can you take?

2 **Be prepared.** Copy and fill out the form on page 197 for lobbying by testifying. This will help you to organize your thoughts and be prepared. (You can speak alone, or several of you can divide the speech into parts and each take a part.) Bring copies of your flyer, too.

3 **Keep it short.** Several short speeches (one to three minutes each) are better than one long, boring speech. Following the testifying form can help you limit yourself.

You may add supporting material, but only if it's necessary. Lawmakers appreciate brief, concise statements.

4 **Dress conservatively.** Remember that your smile is the most impressive thing you can wear (and the most persuasive).

5 **Always call ahead before leaving to testify.** Schedules change suddenly. The discussion of your bill could be delayed.

6 **Arrive on time.** When you arrive, sign up to testify, unless your sponsor does it for you.

7 **Stay on your subject.** If a committee member asks you a question you don't fully understand, simply restate your purpose. Don't argue. Whatever you say will go on the record.

8 **Be aware that your issue will be debated openly.** Legislators will discuss both sides.

9 **Ask for the committee's support before you sit down.**

10 **Send thank-you notes.** Later, send thank-you notes to your sponsor and the committee members.

⸺⸺> IMPORTANT <⸺⸺

If a committee member asks you if you would accept a change in the bill, say that you must talk with your group before you can answer that question.

Marquis Maggiefield and Ho Nguyen, fifth graders at Anderson Open School in Minneapolis, testified before the Minnesota K-12 education finance committee to support a bill that would expand a school breakfast program.

Courtesy the Minnesota legislature

MORE WAYS TO LOBBY

1. **Lobby by letter.** You can send your letter by fax or email to get it there quickly, but sometimes a handwritten letter has more effect. It stands out among all the other correspondence. See pages 32–33 for tips you can use and adapt for this purpose.

2. **Lobby the national government.** You don't have to stop at the state level. Think big! The process is basically the same as for lobbying your state government.

············▶ Check It Out ◀············

Lobbying by Cass R. Sandak (21st Century Books, 1995). An excellent introduction to lobbying from the Inside Government Series. Ages 12 and up.

Special Interests: How Lobbyists Influence Legislation by Jules Archer (Millbrook, 1997). Offers a history of lobbying and an examination of how interest groups try to influence Congress, the White House, and state legislatures. The book deals carefully with both the positive and negative aspects of lobbying. Ages 12 and up.

"You gain strength, courage, and confidence by every experience in which you really stop to look fear in the face. . . . You must do the thing you think you cannot do."
Eleanor Roosevelt

Courtesy Dalie Jimenez

Dalie with Head Start kids.

Dalie Jimenez

Miami, Florida. When Dalie Jimenez learned in psychology class that reading to young children helps their brains develop, she wondered about disadvantaged kids. Did their parents have the books or the time to read to them? Did they get enough attention to get a good head start?

And that's exactly where Dalie's wondering landed her—at a Miami Head Start program. (Head Start is a federal program designed to help disadvantaged preschoolers keep pace with other kids their age.) Dalie, then 14, went there to volunteer. Before she went, she told her club, Future Homemakers of America (FHA) Heroes, about her idea, and about 30 of her friends joined her.

"We created a library for the children," Dalie said, "mostly from donated books. We read to the kids and used puppets to act out stories. We baked goodies for them."

A few years later, in 1995, when she heard that Head Start's funding was about to be cut by a third, Dalie knew she had to do something. That huge cut would practically destroy the program. She decided to lobby to restore funding.

Dalie and her friends made 600 paper dolls to send to politicians. They wrote on the dolls: "Don't give up Head Start." She went to the legislative hearing in her state and spoke to the senators, lobbied, and handed out flyers, all aimed at convincing the lawmakers not to allow the huge cut in funding.

Then with the help of FHA, Dalie went to the U.S. Congress to lobby in person. She followed up by writing a letter to the editor of the *Miami Herald*.

Dalie and her friends weren't the only ones who cared. The media publicized the problem in magazines and newspapers. Such efforts started a chain reaction of protest against cutting funding.

The result of all this combined outrage? The lawmakers did *not* cut the funding and the program was saved. When Dalie heard the good news, she hugged her FHA friends. Then she went back to Head Start and hugged her little friends, who reached up, touched her hair, climbed on her lap, and begged for another story, not understanding that this dedicated young volunteer had just helped to shape their future.

RESOLUTIONS

Resolutions aren't just those wonderful plans for self-improvement you make on New Year's Day and forget the day after. Resolutions can be used to change policies in your city, state, and nation.

There are two main types of resolutions:

1. **A formal statement** urging a plan of action. For example, a legislator may decide to ask a committee to investigate seat belt safety.

   Kids can also initiate a resolution in either the house or the senate.

2. **A commendation** of appreciation. For example, a mayor might make a resolution recognizing the contributions of an individual or group.

At the state level, resolutions can begin in the house, the senate, or the governor's office. Or the house and the senate may write a *joint resolution* together. Add the governor to the house and the senate, and you've got a *concurrent resolution.*

Resolutions have no *binding effect.* In other words, they are not laws. However, Jackson kids began the initiative process with a resolution proposing a Utah State Superfund. Their resolution was made into House Bill 199. The kids lobbied legislators to vote for their bill, and it became a law. Later, the city council and mayor gave the kids a commendation for their work.

If they can do it, so can you.

> **"Resolve to create a good future. It's where you'll spend the rest of your life."**
> **Charles Franklin Kettering**

TIPS FOR SUCCESSFUL RESOLUTIONS

1 Start by contacting your state senator or representative. He'll work with you if he's interested in your idea. You could also initiate your resolution with a staff person or with your governor, but your best bet is your legislator.

2 Your resolution *must not conflict with existing laws and rules.* Your legislator can help you find out if yours would pass.

3 Because resolutions may cost several hundreds of dollars of taxpayer money to process, some legislators grow impatient with the time they require. Don't let this stop you from using this process. Just be sure that your cause is worthwhile.

4 If you're involved in a citywide or statewide campaign for a issue that affects many people, get local governments involved. By doing this, you'll build a strong coalition of support.

Many cities and towns present resolutions in their local meetings. If they are approved there, they will probably be introduced in the next lawmaking session. Include every group or agency you think might be interested in your resolution.

5 Be aware that resolutions are open to debate—people might argue against them. Your resolution might be amended or changed by legislators. Don't take any of this personally.

HOW TO WRITE A RESOLUTION

Resolutions follow a very specific form. Yours will get better attention if you show that you know the form:

- Put your resolution in writing.

- Keep it concise.

- Double-space or triple-space to allow for notes or changes.

- Number the lines for easy reference.

A resolution has two parts: the *preamble* and the *conclusion*. The preamble states the need and reasons for your resolution. The conclusion is based on the reasons given in the preamble.

1. Writing the preamble.

- State the need and reasons for your resolution.

- Start each clause (reason) with *Whereas, The . . .*

- You may write more than one clause.

- End each clause with a comma or a semicolon followed by the word *and.* The last clause should end with *therefore* or *therefore, be it . . .*

2. Writing the conclusion.

- Write your conclusion in statement form. Start with <u>*Resolved, That*</u> . . .

- You may write more than one concluding statement. If you do, the first concluding statement should end, *and be it further.*

- Each statement that follows the first should begin <u>*Resolved, That*</u> . . .

- The statement just before the final conclusion should end *and be it finally . . .*

- <u>*Resolved*</u> must be underlined and followed with a comma. The word *That* must begin with a capital T.

All underlining, punctuation, and sentence structure must remain consistent throughout the resolution.

When your legislator presents your resolution, he will take the floor and state, "I move the adoption of the following resolution," or "I offer the following resolution." Then he will read your resolution and hand it to the chairperson.

You can copy and use the resolution form on page 198 to write your own resolution. Find an example of a real resolution on the next page.

Here's an example:

1 Whereas, The . . . [text of the first pre-amble clause], and

2 Whereas, The . . . [text of the second preamble clause], and

3 Whereas, The . . . [text of the last pre-amble clause]; therefore, be it

4 <u>Resolved,</u> That . . . [stating the action to be taken], and be it further

5 <u>Resolved,</u> That . . . [stating further action to be taken], and be it finally

6 <u>Resolved,</u> That . . . [stating still further action to be taken]. ·······················

Resolution

We the students at Jackson Elementary would like to initiate the following resolution:

1 Whereas, Hazardous waste is defined as wastes that are harmful to living things or environment when improperly handled; and

2 Whereas, The State of Utah has no state superfund to clean up hazardous waste; and

3 Whereas, The State of Utah has approximately 152 sites on the CERCLA list of sites to be investigated; and

4 Whereas, The State of Utah has ten sites on the National Priorities List awaiting cleanup; and

5 Whereas, In the State of Utah in 1986, 3,000,000 tons of hazardous waste was handled by treatment, storage, and disposal; therefore be it

6 <u>Resolved</u>, That the State of Utah create a State Contributory Superfund designated for cleanup of hazardous waste to which a party can voluntarily donate money.

NATIONAL LAWS

You know that kids can make a difference at the local level. Even at the state level. But at the *national* level? Isn't that totally out of reach?

Absolutely not! Kids across the United States have achieved national goals. Jackson kids lobbied the national government to get kids included in the America the Beautiful Act of 1990. Because of their efforts, youth groups across the United States could apply for matching grants of money to improve their neighborhoods.

Maybe you have an idea for a new national law. Or maybe you know an old one that needs changing. Why not give it a try? You've got nothing to lose and much to gain from the experience.

Remember that constituents—people like you, your parents and neighbors, your teachers and friends—are a great source of ideas for initiating new laws or changing old laws.

LEARN ABOUT THE U.S. GOVERNMENT

The United States government has three branches:

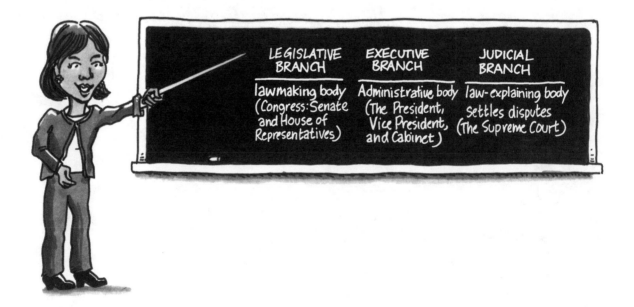

Have you been learning about the U.S. government in school? If not, now's the time—especially if you're thinking about initiating or changing a national law. You need to know what you're talking about!

..........▶ Check It Out ◀..........

These books are written especially for kids:

The Congress by Leslie Gourse (Franklin Watts, 1994). Offers young adult readers and introduction to Congress and how it works.

Congressional Committees by Cass R. Sandak (21st Century Books, 1995). Discusses the committee system as a whole, how committees work and function, Senate and House committees, and the pros and cons of the present system. Ages 12 and up.

Take a Stand: Everything You Never Wanted to Know About Government by Daniel Weizmann, illustrated by Jack Keely (Price Stern Sloan, 1996). Describes how the U.S. government works and how to get involved in politics. Ages 9-12.

These two Web sites can link you to a wealth of government information:

GPO Access
http://www.access.gpo.gov
The site serves as a gateway to Congressional directories, the Congressional Record, the Federal Register, the U.S. Government Manual, a catalog of U.S. government publications, and other federal government resources.

UCLA Youth Enhancement Service
http://www.yes.ucla.edu/voices/
This site, designed to be used by young people, contains a Congressional directory and email links to Congress, as well as links to a wealth of federal government resources.

You can also browse many government resource books at your library reference desk:

The Congressional Directory (U.S. Government Printing Office, published annually). Listings and information about members of Congress and their staffs. This information is also available online:
http://www.senate.gov http://www.house.gov

The Congressional Record (U.S. Government Printing Office, published daily). Tells what happens in Congress each day (bills introduced, bills voted on, hearings scheduled, etc.). This information is also available online:
http://thomas.loc.gov

Encyclopedia of Governmental Advisory Organizations (Gale Research, 1997) A guide to over 5,400 committees, including presidential, Congressional, and public advisory committees, government-related boards, panels, commissions, task forces, conferences, more. Find the most recent volume.

The Federal Register (U.S. Government Printing Office, published daily). Information about executive and agency meetings, rule making, hearings, comment periods, etc. This information is available online:
http://www.access.gpo.gov/su_docs/aces/

The United States Government Manual (U.S. Government Printing Office, published annually). Tells how the federal government is organized, describes duties of different offices, etc. Available online:
http://www.access.gpo.gov/nara

HOW TO INITIATE OR CHANGE A NATIONAL LAW

Suppose you have chosen a problem and researched it. Your solution is to work for a new national law, or a change in an existing law. (Take another look at "Ten Tips for Taking Social Action" on pages 12–13.) Here's how to do it.

1 Contact someone who can help you. If you wanted to initiate or change a state law, you'd contact someone in state government. If your goal is to affect a national law, you'll need someone in national government on your side.

ASK FOR ADVICE (AND WRITE IT DOWN)

As you're looking for people to help you, take time to ask for their opinions and advice on your project. Do they think your idea is a good one? Why or why not? Do you need to change anything to make it work? Get names, phone numbers, and addresses of other people who might help you.

---

a. **Contact a member of Congress.** These are the real lawmakers in national government. And you will eventually need a member of Congress to sponsor your bill.

The best person to pick is someone who represents you. Every state has two senators, and you could pick one of these. Or you could choose a representative instead. How many representatives your state has depends on your state's population. For example, if you live in Maine, you have two representatives; if you live in California, you have as many as 45.

You could also choose a member of Congress who is on a committee that is studying your issue (housing, transportation, etc.). Even though this person might not represent your state, she still might be willing to help you. To be polite, you should tell your senators and representatives if this is what you plan to do.

b. **Contact the president, vice president, or a cabinet member.** These people can't make any laws, but they can suggest changes. And they can offer advice and support. If you can convince any of them to join your team, they will be powerful players.

c. **Contact a staff person or cabinet department member.** As in state government, these are the workers and researchers. They might be easier for you to reach, and they can help you begin the process of initiating or changing a law.

••••••▶ Check It Out ◀••••••

Pick Up the Phone!

- If you'd like to speak to members of Congress, committees, or subcommittees, call the U.S. Capitol at (202) 224-3121

- To find out the status of legislation and dates of hearings, call (202) 225-1772, and ask for the department you want to speak to.

- If you'd like to leave a message for the president, call the White House at (202) 456-1414.

Addresses and phone numbers for other government offices are found on pages 152–155.

2 **Build support for your bill.** Find other people to join your team: other kids, schools, state officials, agencies, media people. You could conduct surveys to find out how other people think (see pages 52–54), and pass petitions to gather names of people who agree with you (see pages 58–60). Try to get media coverage for your cause. (See pages 74–80 for tips, ideas, and examples.) Convincing TV and newspaper reporters to tell your story will usually encourage all sorts of people to support your efforts.

3 **Work with your opposition.** You should never neglect this step! There will always be people with different needs and people who disagree with you. Ignoring them might keep you from reaching your goal. It might also keep you from discovering what you have in common, and maybe even joining forces to work together.

At the very least, you might be able to convince these people not to interfere with what you're trying to do. And you'll learn to see their side of the issue, too.

4 **Lobby for your legislation.** Try to convince lawmakers to support your bill or proposed change. You can lobby by phone, letter, fax, or email if you have access to an email account.

Lobbying in person might seem difficult without a private plane. Then again, Audrey Chase flew to Washington, D.C., and lobbied in person for the "Leaf it to Us" tree amendment. (You read Audrey's story on page 10.)

Kids have flown all over the country and even internationally to work on problems. How do they finance their travels? Usually they find sponsors to pay their expenses—supporters in business or industry. Or they raise funds in other ways.

> **"Congress shall make no law . . . abridging the freedom of speech, or of the press; or the right of the people peaceably to assemble, and to petition the government for a redress of grievances."**
>
> **First Amendment, Constitution of the United States, 1791.**

"LEAF it to US!"

Jackson Elementary
750 W. 200 N.
Salt Lake City, U.t.
84116

The President
The White House
Washington D.C. 20500

Dear President Bush:

Hi! We would like money for kids to plant trees on public grounds across the nation. We heard you want to put up $60,000,000 for planting trees. That's exactly what we would like to do. Could some of it be used for a Children's Fund for kids across the nation?

Kids could match 10 to 20% of the money they took out. The kids could apply for grants. The money could be kept in Washington D.C.

We would not like to use an Adult fund, we would like it to be just for kids.

<u>One tree</u> in it's average 50 yr. lifetime contributes $162,000 worth of air pollution control. They also recycle water, and prevent soil erosion.

We've already talked to the honorable Senator Orrin Hatch and asked him to pass some legislation or set aside some money for kids. We're already planting trees in Utah. We have already gone to our own legislature.

Is there anything more we can do?

Trees are a Tree-mendous Con-Tree-bution!

Sincerely,

Shane Price   Audrey Chase
Jeremy Maestas   Micki J Nay   Darren P.
Sharee Bright   Richelle Warner
Shannon Ackman   Richard Tehero

THE WHITE HOUSE
WASHINGTON

April 25, 1990

Dear Girls and Boys:

Senator Orrin Hatch was kind enough to write to me about your wonderful "Leaf-It-To-Us — Children's Crusade for Trees Project." As I read the material from you, your principal, and the Senator, I was impressed by your creativity and initiative. Your enthusiasm and hard work are an example for all Americans to follow.

As you watch your trees grow, you will be able to take great pride in the contribution you have made to improving our environment. Your forestry project represents a lasting investment in the future.

Mrs. Bush joins me in commending you for your efforts. You can be certain that we will tell others of the time, effort, and energy you have put into this worthy project. Keep up the good work, and God bless you.

Sincerely,

George Bush

Pupils of Jackson Elementary School
Extended Learning Program
750 West 200 North
Salt Lake City, Utah 84116

AMENDING THE U.S. CONSTITUTION

The United States Constitution is an amazing document. Written more than 200 years ago, its rules still govern the nation. Every law that's passed must be in accordance with the principles laid out in the Constitution.

Suppose the solution to your problem is to try to amend (change) the Constitution. This is *very* difficult to accomplish—but that doesn't mean it's impossible.

Are you interested? Some kids are.

There are two basic ways an amendment can be proposed to the Constitution of the United States:

1 **Congress can propose an amendment with a $2/3$ vote of both houses.** For an amendment to be accepted, it must be approved by

- $3/4$ of the state legislatures, or
- conventions in $3/4$ of the states.

2 **Legislatures of $2/3$ of the states can call a convention for proposing amendments.** For an amendment to be accepted, it must be approved by

- $3/4$ of the state legislatures, or
- conventions in $3/4$ of the states.

In the history of the United States, more than 10,000 amendments have been suggested. Only 33 of these proposed amendments have been approved by Congress. And only 26 amendments—including the 10 amendments in the Bill of Rights—have been approved by the states.

So, how do you start the long, slow process? As a kid, you could begin by contacting a member of Congress from your state. But you should probably collect thousands of signatures on a petition to show support for your amendment. You could also start by contacting the president, the vice president, or a staff person, just as you would to initiate or change a law.

Some fifth graders in New Jersey have tried to amend the Constitution. Here is their amazing story.

..........► Check It Out ◄..........

The H-Files
http://www.pbs.org/point/pie/h-files

This Web site hosted by PBS offers links to the U.S. Constitution and other important historical documents, such as the Declaration of Independence, Lincoln's Emanicipation Proclamation, and many more.

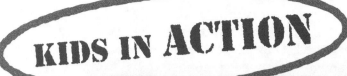

Courtesy *U.S. News & World Report*

Teacher Nick Byrne and his KAP students state their case for environmental education in the New York Assembly Standing Committee on Environmental Conservation in Albany, New York.

Kids Against Pollution (KAP)

Closter, New Jersey. While studying the Bill of Rights, a group of energetic fifth graders in teacher Nick Byrne's class lifted their noses from their books to ask, "How can we use our right to free expression?"

"Choose a topic and write to newspapers, magazines, and public officials," Byrne answered.

Since pollution seemed to cloud the pages of everything they read, Byrne's students chose that as their project. But they weren't satisfied with just writing letters. These kids at Tenakill School in Closter, New Jersey, went a bit further than that.

In 1987, they founded a networking information organization called KAP—Kids Against Pollution. They created their own logo and motto:

"Save the Earth—not just for us but for future generations."

That's how KAP got started. Since then, KAP kids have carried their environmental message to thousands of kids around the country and around the world through sending out massive mailings, distributing environmental information, and providing workshops for kids. Chapters of KAP have sprung up all around the United States and in places as far away from KAP's beginnings as Africa, Siberia, and China.

KAP kids also advocate the passage of an amendment to the U.S. Constitution, stating that everyone has the right to clean air, water, and land; safe energy; and the preservation of biodiversity. Does that sound impossible? Actually, it's an uphill climb, but not impossible. New Jersey Representative Frank Pallone has expressed interest in sponsoring their bill. But it's no easy job to make an amendment to the Constitution.

They have more help. Ralph Nader, best known for his work protecting the rights of consumers, has offered to donate a Web site service for them.

In 1997, a coalition of KAP kids and their new advisor, Christine Shahin-Wood, went to New York to lobby Congress members and gather support for their project. They encourage groups of kids across the country to get resolutions passed in their own states and to send a copy to KAP. When they have collected enough state and local resolutions, they will present the package to Congress and lobby the lawmakers to pass the amendment.

You can also sign their petition on 136 and mail it to KAP.

From a new Jersey classroom to a Constitutional amendment may seem impossibly far to go. But the KAP kids are trying it. They call it "free expression." How are you going to express yourself?

Kids Against Pollution's Environmental Bill of Rights

"Save The Earth, Not Just For Us
But For Future Generations"

Our legislators are bound by law in the Preamble of our Constitution to provide for our general welfare. Therefore, we are entitled by law to clean air, land, water and all life forms present therein. Our rights to such an environment are not being upheld, therefore we propose this amendment to our state and federal constitutions. Those who have pledged to uphold the Constitution are duly bound to enact and enforce the law, thereby ensuring our right to a clean, safe, and biodiverse environment.

We the children, claim the right to receive what Nature intended to bestow.

Air
We have the right to clean air, free of harmful substances. Respiratory diseases continue to increase, such as asthma, in children. Chlorofluorocarbons and carbon monoxide continue to contribute to global warming ("greenhouse effect"). Clean air is essential for life and health and must not be compromised.

Water
We have the right to uncontaminated drinking water. 1% of the world's water is fresh water. This 1% is increasingly polluted with toxins and other harmful substances, such as mercury, PCs, lead, and dioxin. Our nation's waterways are used as dumping grounds. In New York State alone, there are fifty-five lakes and streams from which citizens can not eat the fish. Water is the life blood of our planet and must not be compromised.

Land
We have the right to soil free from contaminants. Our natural resources are exploited and depleted, only to end up discarded. The federal Environmental Protection Agency admits that even double lined state-of-the-art landfills "eventually leak." Groundwater, air and soil are at stake. Our land is a precious resource and must be protected. Reduction of the waste stream is vital. Recycling and reuse must be mandatory for the quality of life to be restored. An alternative, environmentally concerned work-force is essential for economic and environmental security.

Energy
We have the right to safe, unpolluting forms of energy. Non-renewable resources and fossil fuels continue to contribute to pollution and environmental degradation. Nuclear waste is deadly; radioactive poisoning of streams, lakes and soil increase daily. Controversy surrounds the effects of electromagnetic fields. Technology exists today able to replace these outdated harmful practices, out struggle to survive because present energy producers control the energy market. Alternative safe energy methods must be made easily available to the average citizen.

The Natural World
We have the right to share our habitat with all the life forms it supports. All forms of life are interconnected (also known as the "web of life") as food and/or medicine for others. Humans benefit from other forms of life not only for food & medicine, but are keenly responsive to Nature's beauty gaining immaterial profits. Ancient trees and all other forms of flora and fauna must have sanctuary. The rights of existence are intrinsic to all other life forms as well as humans. Biodiversity must be safeguarded. Future generations have the right to experience & embrace life's diversity.

Education
Environmental Education is necessary to continue to instill environmental awareness. Environmental Education should be a separate course beginning in kindergarten, culminating at graduation with a special recognition award. Curriculum must emphasize conservation, alternative technologies, and problem solving.

By signing this petition, I urge our State and Federal governments to adopt KAP's Environmental Bill of Rights as an Amendment to the United States Constitution and the constitution of all fifty states.

_____   _____
Signature   Address

I want to help pass KAP's amendment! Let me know what I can do!

Kids Against Pollution, PO Box 22, Newport, NY 13416 • Phone: (315) 891-3288 • email: kap@borg.com

Environmental Bill of Rights Petition

"Save The Earth, Not Just For Us But For Future Generations"

We the undersigned fully support Kids Against Pollution (KAP) in their effort to have their Environmental Bill of Rights adopted by both the state and national constitutions. The areas addressed: AIR – WATER – LAND – SAFE ENERGY – BIODIVERSITY & EDUCATION, are important. Together WE can "Save The Earth, Not Just For Us But For Future Generations."

Name   **Address**

_____   _____

_____   _____

_____   _____

_____   _____

_____   _____

_____   _____

_____   _____

_____   _____

_____   _____

_____   _____

_____   _____

_____   _____

_____   _____

Remember to:
1. Photocopy, 2. Sign and have your friends sign, 3. Send to: PO Box 22, Newport, NY 13416
Email: kap@borg.com Phone: (315) 891-3288

137

THE COURTS:
INTERPRETING THE LAWS

> **"We are under a Constitution, but the Constitution is what the judges say it is."**
>
> **Charles Evans Hughes, American jurist**

The courts are the third branch of government. Courts exist to interpret the laws: they decide how the laws will be applied when cases are brought to court. In the U.S. there are two court systems: *state* and *federal*. State courts are established by state constitutions, and federal courts are established by the U.S. Constitution. Both state courts and federal courts have several levels. The lowest level is the *trial* level. At this level, judges conduct the trial to determine if a law has been broken. The next level is the *appeals* level. Appeals courts review the decisions made by the lower courts and determine if the law was interpreted accurately. The *Supreme Court* is at the highest level. The Supreme Court hears

cases to interpret laws that have been challenged. It asks, Does this law violate the Constitution?

People can't lobby courts the way they lobby lawmakers, although strong public opinion is bound to have some effect on how laws are interpreted. (That's why people protest decisions such as those allowing or opposing the death penalty.)

There are many other ways to affect the judicial system with your social action projects. Mock trials, youth courts, school courts, conflict resolution, child advocacy—these are only some ideas that many other kids have used to learn about the impact they can have.

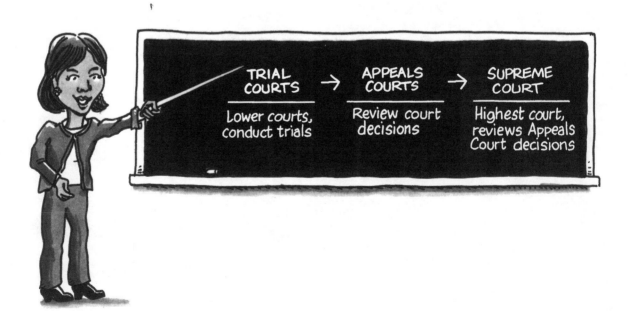

TRIAL COURTS → APPEALS COURTS → SUPREME COURT

Lower courts, conduct trials | Review court decisions | Highest court, reviews Appeals Court decisions

············▶ **Check It Out** ◀···········

Putting on Mock Trials, edited by Richard L. Roe (ABA Publications, 1996). This book produced by the American Bar Association (ABA) has resources for setting up mock trials for elementary and secondary students.

MOCK TRIALS

Mock trials are imaginary court cases that allow young people to experience legal procedures through role play. For example, you can put Hansel and Gretel on trial for murder. Or put Goldilocks on trial for breaking and entering. Or maybe you'd like to write something closer to real life, such as putting a teenage shoplifter on trial.

Mock trials are challenging and fun. By planning and participating in mock trials, you can better learn how the court system works and what happens when people are tried for breaking laws. There are many kits available for setting up mock trials. But it can also be fun to set up the imaginary experience by writing the history of the case yourself. You can assign people to play various roles: judge, defendant, prosecuting attorney, defense attorney, witnesses, experts, bailiffs, clerks, jurors. Allow time afterwards for discussion and analysis.

Mock trials are just one way to learn about working with the judicial system. Kids all over the country are working with courts on social action projects. Here are a few other ideas you can try yourself.

·····················▶

YOUTH COURTS

Sixteen-year-old Anna bites her nails as she awaits the jury's decision. She has been charged with possession of alcohol. But her jury is not made up of adults, such as a construction worker, a nurse, and an electrician. Her jury consists of other teenagers: Jessica, Neil, and Curtis, who serve in Teen Court. The jury accepts Anna's plea—guilty—and sentences her to 30 hours of community service, an alcohol education class, and duty on a future jury for Teen Court. Despite the sentence, Anna smiles with relief. She is glad she didn't have to be tried in juvenile court, where a judge would likely have imposed a big fine and she would have received a juvenile criminal record as well.

According to the American Bar Association, at the beginning of 1997 there were 276 youth courts in the United States operating in 33 states, and the movement is growing. They are becoming more common for many reasons. Two of the most important are that (1) they hold young people accountable for their actions, and (2) they give young people an opportunity to learn about both the law and solving problems effectively. These courts are headed by adult judges or attorneys, but the jurors, attorneys, bailiffs, and clerks (and sometimes the judges) are all under age 19.

Youth courts are usually designed to try young people who have been charged with a minor crime for the first time. This often involves crimes such as underage drinking, drug use, theft, vandalism, or disorderly conduct. In communities with youth courts, young defendants have the opportunity to be sentenced by a jury of their peers. Defendants who complete their sentence have the charges dropped from their record.

Teen courts are designed a bit differently in each community. Most require defendants to plead guilty or *nolo contendore* (Latin for "I won't contest the charge"). A

⊶▶ Check It Out ◀⊷

American Bar Association
National Law-Related Education Resource Center
541 North Fairbanks Court
Chicago, IL 60611-3314
Tel.: (312) 988-6386
Fax: (312) 988-5032
Email: pnessel@staff.abanet.org
http://www.abanet.org/
The ABA also has a library of law-related education resources, activities, and booklets, including *Resolving Conflicts, Influencing Public Policy,* and much more. Ask for a catalog of their resources and materials on teen courts.

American Probation and Parole Association
Teen Courts Project Manager
c/o The Council of State Governments
PO Box 11910
Lexington, KY 40578-1910
(606) 244-8215
This organization offers a packet of information on creating teen courts in your community.

Juvenile Justice Clearinghouse
1-800-638-8736
http://www.ncjrs.org/ojjhome.htm
Offers the publication "Peer Justice and Youth Empowerment: An Implementation Guide for Teen Court Programs." Call the toll-free number to get the print version, or visit the Web site to read the full text online.

The Teen Court Homepage
http://tqd.advanced.org/2640
This site by the Knox County (Illinois) teen court offers a teen court manual that you can download free.

Youth Court National Home Page
http://www.projectfind.com/youthcourt.html
Includes a live chat room and youth court listings by state, as well as links to other sites.

few teen courts, however, do rule on the guilt or innocence of defendants who plead not guilty.

Youth courts are usually set up in one of two ways: (1) a trial model, or (2) a peer jury model. Trial-model teen courts use young people as volunteer attorneys who question witnesses and present the facts of the case to the teen jury and judge. The judge is usually an adult volunteer, although in some teen courts, a young person who has served as an attorney for some time may become a judge. In a peer-jury court, there are no teen attorneys to question the defendant and witnesses; the jury questions the defendant directly and determines the sentence.

SCHOOL COURTS

If setting up a teen court in your community is not for you, you might start smaller. Work to set up a court in your school to try students who break *school* rules.

You can follow some of the guidelines for teen court programs. Or you might use these tips in setting up a school court:

1 **Write a proposal for a school court** (see page 45). Present your proposal to the principal. If the principal likes the idea, ask for a slot on a faculty meeting agenda, and present the proposal to the faculty. If you get a go-ahead, you still have a lot of work to do.

2 **Find a sponsor** among the teachers.

> **"The firm basis of government is justice, not pity."**
> **Woodrow Wilson**

3 **Set up the space** for the court.

- Gather all the materials you might need: paper, pencils, forms, envelopes, a large calendar for recording dates of trials.

- Find a place to store things.

- Arrange a quiet location with chairs for holding court.

4 **Write rules for court procedures.** This should be done as a team including students, your sponsor, and perhaps parents. Try to get all the different participants to agree on the procedures.

- When will court take place? How often?

- Who will be tried by the school court?

- Who will be judges? Adults or students? If students, what will be the requirements for serving as a judge? You might ask the principal or sponsoring teacher to select several judges to serve on a rotating basis. The principal, judges, your sponsor, and you might become the School Court Operating Committee.

- Who else will serve on the court? Jurors? Will there be prosecutors, defense attorneys, bailiffs, clerks, a court reporter? (Filling all these roles requires very mature students.) How will court personnel be selected?

- What kind of training will students receive?

- What types of cases will the court hear? The principal or your sponsor needs to be involved in deciding which cases will be tried in School Court. An adult sponsor should be present at all trials.

- List offenses and the penalties for first mistakes, second, and so on.

- List the penalties for breaking specific rules: school service hours, loss of privileges, in-school detention, and so on.

- List the rewards and privileges for improved behavior.

- List the consequences of not completing penalties.

- Will you accept only cases where students admit their guilt, and the court then determines the penalty? Or will students be allowed to plead guilty or not guilty? If a student pleads not guilty, will the judgment be made by the judge or the jury?

- Who will inform the rule breaker of the consequences?

- When will follow-up sessions be scheduled?

- How will rule breakers show they have completed their consequences?

5 **Set up a mock trial** to run through your procedures. Is there anything you forgot to consider? If there is, go back and refine your written procedures before you hold an actual session of the School Court.

6 **Create a court handbook** that lists procedures and the responsibilities that come with each role. Example:

Responsibilities of the Judge

- Keep the trial confidential. You don't tell other people about the details.

- Set up the courtroom with the sponsor and bring in everyone who needs to be there.

- Call the court to order.

- No name calling. The judge should always be polite.

- Follow all school court procedures.

- Fill out a student court chart (see page 199) for each person found to have broken the rules. Be sure to add a date for a follow-up to see that the penalty was completed. Keep a copy of the chart for the court records and make a photocopy for the rule breaker.

- Write the date on your calendar for the follow-up trial.

- Contact the sponsor and the rule breaker two days ahead of the follow-up trial as a reminder.

- Hold the follow-up to see if the penalty was completed. If it has been, you may restore privileges; if not, consult your sponsor for further action.

Final considerations: Ask your sponsor to help you make sure that school court does not create factions in your school and that it is used to resolve problems in a positive way that helps kids improve. It should never be used in a way that allows judges or jurors to gang up on rule breakers. Keep it positive.

You might also have a family or club court, following similar procedures.

CONFLICT RESOLUTION & MEDIATION

While youth courts and school courts can handle many problems, the best solution is usually to intercept a conflict before it escalates. Many kids begin social action projects by working to create a conflict resolution program in their schools or clubs. Remember the Conflect Busters at Franklin Elementary School (see page 47) and Marieo Henry's proposal to start a conflict resolution program at Detroit's Westside Athletic Club (see page 64)?

These kids saw the importance of acting quickly before small problems grew into big ones.

Does your school offer a conflict resolution program? If not, you could encourage your school administrators to make conflict resolution training available to students, teachers, and staff. Several organizations offer great conflict resolution and conflict mediation techniques.

While successful mediation takes practice, you can learn to help people solve their conflict before it gets out of hand. The Resolving Conflict Creatively Program offers a list of steps (see the next page).

⸺► Check It Out ◄⸺

Educators for Social Responsibility
Resolving Conflict Creatively Program
23 Garden Street
Cambridge, MA 02138
(617) 492-1764
http://www.benjerry.com/esr/
The Resolving Conflict Creatively Program (RCCP) teaches thousands of teachers and students in schools nationwide how to respond nonviolently to conflict. The "Steps for Mediation" on page 143 are from RCCP. If you visit the website (hosted by Ben & Jerry's Ice Cream), click on "RCCP," then click on "Kids' Conscience Acts of Peace Project" for activities you can print out and distribute in your school, and on "Kids Keeping the Peace" for tips, games, activities, and success stories.

National School Safety Center
4165 Thousand Oaks Blvd., Suite 290
Westlake Village, CA 91362
(805) 373-9977
http://www.nssc1.org/

Safe and Drug-Free Schools Program
1250 Maryland Ave., SW, Portals 604
Washington, DC 20202
(202) 260-6722
http://www.ed.gov/offices.OESE/SDFS/

Introduction

1. Introduce yourself as a mediator.
2. Ask those in the conflict if they would like your help in solving the problem.
3. Find a quiet area to hold the mediation.
4. Ask for agreement to the following:
   - try to solve the problem
   - no name calling
   - let the other person finish talking
   - confidentiality

Listening

5. Ask the first person "What happened?" Paraphrase.
6. Ask the first person how she or he feels. Reflect the feelings.
7. Ask the second person "What happened?" Paraphrase.
8. Ask the second person how he or she feels. Reflect the feelings.

Looking for Solutions

9. Ask the first person what she or he could have done differently. Paraphrase.
10. Ask the second person what she or he could have done differently. Paraphrase.
11. Ask the first person what she or he can do here and now to help solve the problem. Paraphrase.
12. Ask the second person what she or he can do here and now to help solve the problem. Paraphrase.
13. Use creative questioning to bring disputants closer to a solution.

Finding Solutions

14. Help both disputants find a solution they feel good about.
15. Repeat the solution and all of its parts to both disputants and ask if each agrees.
16. Congratulate both people on a successful mediation.

KIDS IN COURT

If you really want to put on your social action gloves, Kids in Court is for you. Kids in Court is a program that allows mature teenagers and adults to help abused children navigate the court process. Its purpose is to ensure that child victims who testify in court have an advocate or protector. The interrogations and testifying can be terrifying to a child. Teen volunteers are trained to help. Here's what they learn to do:

- Explain to the child what will happen in the testifying process.

- Help the child understand the role of a witness in a criminal trial.

- Teach the child about the roles of key people in the courtroom.

- Offer comfort and understanding.

- Instruct the child on how to testify.

- Help the child role-play testifying in the actual courtroom.

- Appear in court with the child (and even sometimes hold the child's hand).

- Provide a chance for parents of the victim to talk with a parent of a former child witness, if appropriate.

......► Check It Out ◄......

Guide to American Law: Everyone's Legal Encyclopedia (West Publishing Company, supplemented annually). If you enjoy reading about landmark laws, look for this book at your library reference desk or local law library. It's written in language even nonlawyers can understand.

What Are My Rights? 95 Questions and Answers About Teens and the Law by Thomas A. Jacobs, J.D. (Free Spirit Publishing, 1997). Lets teens know about the laws that affect them—so they can make informed decisions about what they should and shouldn't do.

Kids in Court offers teens a great opportunity to help a child in need as well as to learn more about how the law and the court system work.

HINTS FOR SETTING UP KIDS IN COURT

1 If your community doesn't already have a Kids in Court program, you might want to start one. Find an adult who could help you. A good place to start is with a parent, a teacher, or a club or religious leader.

2 Send for information on how the program works. You wouldn't need to make your program be exactly the same. Contact:

> **Kids in Court**
> Exploited Children's Help Organization
> 2440 Grinstead Drive
> Louisville, KY 40204
> (502) 458-9997

3 Find a sponsor who works in the court system. A good person to start with is the *victim advocate* in the prosecutor's office. Almost every court system has a person designated as an advocate for victims. This person will usually make a fine sponsor and will know how to complete all the remaining steps.

4 Get funding for the program for supplies and operating costs.

5 Set up an office location or place to work from.

6 Plan a training program.

7 Advertise for volunteers.

8 Set up a rotating schedule for teen volunteers in court.

KIDS IN ACTION

Mercedes Jones hugs a child she has helped through "Kids in Court"

Mercedes Jones

Louisville, Kentucky. As a child, Mercedes Jones was sexually abused in her daycare home. For four years, between the ages of three and seven, she endured this molestation from the husband of the daycare provider. When she struggled, he pressed a knife against her throat or held a gun to her temple, threatening her that he would kill her mother and brother if she told anyone.

When Mercedes was eight years old, she broke through the dam of fear and silence when her mom shared a newspaper article with her, which told of a child who had been abused. Mercedes cried out the whole story to her mom.

Through tender discussion with her mom and help from a child psychiatrist, Mercedes decided to bring charges and to testify against her abuser. It took tremendous courage, because by pressing charges, everyone found out what had happened to her—including Mercedes's friends, who treated her as if she had a disease. She transferred to a private school where she could start anew.

Meanwhile, four boys who had also been abused by the same man stepped forward to testify as well. The abuser was convicted of five felonies and misdemeanors for molesting children and sentenced to 25 years in prison. Investigators estimated that he had victimized as many as 40 children. He died in prison shortly after.

The nightmare wasn't over for Mercedes, however. She had flashbacks as she grew older and continued to seek counseling. Ever a fighter, Mercedes threw herself into schoolwork and gymnastics and excelled at both.

But her troubled soul still needed another outlet. At 14, Mercedes began volunteering for Exploited Children's Help Organization (ECHO) where her mother worked full-time. She was eventually hired as a coordinator for a program called Kids in Court.

Through Kids in Court, Mercedes helped other children testify in court against the people who had abused them. Mercedes met with the children and taught them about testifying. She walked them through the whole process and explained what would happen during the trial. Sometimes she held their hands the whole time. By showing these abused children the actual courtroom ahead of time and the seat where they would sit to testify, she helped allay some of their fears. She made the process more familiar, and reminded them to look at someone they trusted—a parent, lawyer, psychologist—so they wouldn't be intimidated by the abuser's watchful gaze.

The children often hugged her at the end of the trial for staying with them and letting them know she understood their fears. She gave them the courage to stand up for justice. And at the same time, Mercedes's heart began to heal.

Part 4

RESOURCES

STATE LEGISLATURE CONTACTS:
CAPITALS, ZIP CODES, AND CENTRAL SWITCHBOARDS

State or jurisdiction	Capital	Zip Code	Phone
Alabama	Montgomery	36130	334/242-8000
Alaska	Juneau	99801	907/465-3500
Arizona	Phoenix	85007	602/542-4900
Arkansas	Little Rock	77201	501/682-3000
California	Sacramento	95814	916/322-9900
Colorado	Denver	80203	303/866-5000
Connecticut	Hartford	06106	860-566-2211
Delaware	Dover	19903	302/739-4000
Florida	Tallahassee	32399	904/488-1234
Georgia	Atlanta	30334	404/656-2000
Hawaii	Honolulu	96813	808/548-2211
Idaho	Boise	83720	208/334-2411
Illinois	Springfield	62706	217/782-2000
Indiana	Indianapolis	46204	317/232-3140
Iowa	Des Moines	50319	515/281-5011
Kansas	Topeka	66612	913/296-0111
Kentucky	Frankfort	40601	502/564-3130
Louisiana	Baton Rouge	70804	504/342-6600
Maine	Augusta	04333	207/582-9500
Maryland	Annapolis	21401	410/841-3000
Massachusetts	Boston	02133	617/727-2121
Michigan	Lansing	48909	517/373-1873
Minnesota	St. Paul	55515	612/296-6013
Mississippi	Jackson	39215	601/359-1000
Missouri	Jefferson City	65101	314/751-2000
Montana	Helena	59620	406/444-2511
Nebraska	Lincoln	68509	402/471-2311
Nevada	Carson City	89710	702/687-5000
New Hampshire	Concord	03301	603/271-1110
New Jersey	Trenton	08625	609/292-2121
New Mexico	Santa Fe	87503	505/827-4011
New York	Albany	12224	581/474-2121
North Carolina	Raleigh	17601	919/733-1110
North Dakota	Bismarck	58505	701/328-2000
Ohio	Columbus	43266	614/466-2000
Oklahoma	Oklahoma City	73105	405/521-2011
Oregon	Salem	97310	503/378-3131
Pennsylvania	Harrisburg	17120	717/787-2121
Rhode Island	Providence	02903	401/277-2000
South Carolina	Columbia	29211	803/734-1000
South Dakota	Pierre	57501	605/773-3011
Tennessee	Nashville	37243	615/741-3011
Texas	Austin	78711	512/463-4630
Utah	Salt Lake City	84114	801/538-3000

State or jurisdiction	Capital	Zip Code	Phone
Vermont	Montpelier	05609	802/828-1110
Virginia	Richmond	23219	804/786-0000
Washington	Olympia	98504	206/753-5000
West Virginia	Charleston	25305	304/558-3456
Wisconsin	Madison	53702	608/266-2211
Wyoming	Cheyenne	82002	307/777-7220
District of Columbia	Washington	20004	202/727-1000
American Samoa	Pago Pago	96799	684/633-5231
Federated States of Micronesia	Kolonia	96941	NCS
Guam	Agana	96910	671/472-3461
Marshall Islands	Majuro	96960	NCS
No. Mariana Islands	Saipan	96950	NCS
Puerto Rico	San Juan	00901	809/721-6040
Republic of Belau	Koror	96940	NCS
Virgin Islands	Charlotte Amalie	00801	809/774-0880

THE GOVERNMENT OF THE UNITED STATES

THE CONSTITUTION

EXECUTIVE BRANCH

THE PRESIDENT
Executive Office of the President

White House
Office of Management and Budget
Council of Economic Advisors
National Security Council
Office of Policy Development

Office of National Drug Control Policy
Office of the U.S. Trade Representative
Council on Environmental Quality
Office of Science and Technology Policy
Office of Administration

THE VICE PRESIDENT
Office of the Vice President

LEGISLATIVE BRANCH

THE CONGRESS

Senate   **House**

Architect of the Capitol
United States Botanical Garden
General Accounting Office
Government Printing Office
Library of Congress
United States Tax Court
Congressional Budget Office

JUDICIAL BRANCH

THE SUPREME COURT OF THE UNITED STATES

United States Court of Appeals
United States District Courts
United States Claims Court
United States Court of Appeals
for the Armed Forces
United States Court of Veteran Appeals
Administrative Office of the United States Courts
Federal Judicial Center
United States Sentencing Commission

DEPARTMENT OF AGRICULTURE	DEPARTMENT OF COMMERCE	DEPARTMENT OF DEFENSE	DEPARTMENT OF EDUCATION
DEPARTMENT OF ENERGY	DEPARTMENT OF THE INTERIOR	DEPARTMENT OF JUSTICE	DEPARTMENT OF LABOR
DEPARTMENT OF STATE	DEPARTMENT OF TRANSPORTATION	DEPARTMENT OF THE TREASURY	DEPARTMENT VETERANS AFFAIRS
	DEPARTMENT OF HEALTH AND HUMAN SERVICES	DEPARTMENT OF HOUSING AND URBAN DEVELOPMENT	

From: *United States Government Manual*, 1996/97. Office of the Federal Register, U.S. Government Printing Office, Washington, D.C., p. 21.

U.S. GOVERNMENT OFFICES

EXECUTIVE BRANCH

You can reach the following executive branch offices online through the White House home page:
http://www.whitehouse.gov/

White House Offices

The President of the United States
White House Office
1600 Pennsylvania Ave.
Washington, DC 20500
(202) 456-1414
president@whitehouse.gov

Vice President of the United States
Old Executive Office Bldg.
Washington, DC 20501
(202) 456-2326
vicepresident@whitehouse.gov

Council of Economic Advisers
Old Executive Office Bldg.
Washington, DC 20502
(202) 395-5084
Analyzes the national economy; advises the president on economic policies.

Council on Environmental Quality
Room 360
Old Executive Office Building
Washington, DC 20501
(202) 356-6224
Advises the president on environmental issues.

National Security Council
Old Executive Office Bldg.
Washington, DC 20506
(202) 456-1414
Advises the president on issues involving military and national security.

Office of Management and Budget
Executive Office Bldg.
Washington, DC 20503
(202) 395-3080
Assists and advises the president in managing the executive branch; administers the federal budget.

Office of National Drug Control Policy
Executive Office of the President
Washington, DC 20500
(202) 395-7347
Information on policies to control illegal drugs.

Cabinet Departments

Department of Agriculture
14th Street and Independence Ave., SW
Washington, DC 20250
(202) 720-2791
http://www.usda.gov
Works to market farm products; combats poverty, hunger, and malnutrition; works to improve the environment by protecting the soil, water, forests, etc.

Department of Commerce
14th Street Between Constitution and Pennsylvania Aves., NW
Washington, DC 20230
(202) 482-2000
http://www.doc.gov
Promotes international trade, economic growth, business growth, etc.

Department of Defense
Office of the Secretary
The Pentagon
Washington, DC 20301-1155
(703) 545-6700
http://www.dtic.dla.mil/defenselink/osd/
Provides the country's military forces.

Department of Education
600 Independence Ave., SW
Washington, DC 20202
(202) 708-5366
http://www.ed.gov
  Handles federal assistance to schools and educational programs.

Department of Energy
1000 Independence Ave., SW
Washington, DC 20585
(202) 586-5000
http://www.doe.gov
  Deals with national energy use, including conservation and the nuclear weapons program.

Department of Health and Human Services
200 Independence Ave., SW
Washington, DC 20201
(202) 619-0257
http://www.os.dhhs.gov
  The department most concerned with meeting human needs; deals with health issues, social services, etc.

Department of Housing and Urban Development
451 Seventh Street, SW
Washington, DC 20410
(202) 708-1422
http://www.hud.gov
  Responsible for meeting the nation's housing needs, including insurance, rentals, low-income family dwellings, etc.

Department of the Interior
1849 C Street, NW
Washington, DC 20240
(202) 208-3171
http://www.doi.gov
  Responsible for most of the nationally owned lands and resources, including parks, forests, wildlife, etc.

Department of Justice
Constitution Ave. and 10th Street, NW
Washington, DC 20530
(202) 514-2000
http://www.usdoj.gov
  The largest law firm in the United States; serves as counsel for all citizens. Works to uphold the law, safeguard consumers, etc.

Department of Labor
200 Constitution Ave., NW
Washington, DC 20210
(202) 219-5000
http://www.dol.gov
  Works to improve the nation's employment rates and working conditions

Department of State
2201 C Street, NW
Washington, DC 20520
(202) 647-4000
http://www.state.gov
  Advises the president on foreign policy matters.

Department of Transportation
400 Seventh Street, SW
Washington, DC 20590
(202) 366-4000
http://www.dot.gov
  Makes national policy for highways, mass transit, railroads, airlines, waterways, oil and gas pipelines, etc.

Department of the Treasury
1500 Pennsylvania Ave., NW
Washington, DC 20220
(202) 622-2000
http://www.ustreas.gov
  Sets money policies, including taxes; mints coins and currency.

Department of Veteran Affairs
810 Vermont Ave., NW
Washington, DC 20420
(202) 273-4900
http://www.va.gov
  Operates programs for veterans and their families (education, housing, medical care, etc.).

LEGISLATIVE BRANCH

U.S. Congress

Write directly to individual senators and representatives at these addresses or contact them online:

The Senate
The Capitol
Washington, DC 20510
http://www.senate.gov

The House of Representatives
The Capitol
Washington, DC 20515
http://www.house.gov

Reach any member of Congress and all committees and subcommittees by calling (202) 224-3121.

Legislative Status Office. For information on legislation in the House and the Senate, and for dates of committee hearings, call (202) 225-1772.

Library of Congress—Thomas. You can check information on committees, current bills, voting records, and the Congressional Record at *http://thomas.loc.gov/*

··········▶ Check It Out ◀··········

- Capitol Hill operator: (202) 224-3121. Connects you to the Senate or House of Representatives offices.

- The Yellow Book—Federal numbers: (202) 347-7757.

Congressional Agencies

Congressional Budget Office
Second and D Streets, SW
Washington, DC 20515
(202) 226-2621
http://www.cbo.gov
　　Reports to Congress on the impact of the federal budget.

General Accounting Office
441 G Street, NW
Washington, DC 20548
(202) 512-3000
http://www.gao.gov
　　The investigative arm of Congress; concerned with the use of public money.

Library of Congress
101 Independence Ave., SE
Washington, DC 20540
(202) 707-5000
http://www.loc.gov
　　The national library—HUGE, and housed in many buildings. The Web site offers numerous links to useful information.

FedWorld Information Network
http://www./fedworld.gov/
　　FedWorld was established by the National Technical Information Service, an agency of the U.S. Department of Commerce to provide the public a one-stop location for finding U.S. government information.

U.S. Government Printing Office (GPO)
North Capitol and H Streets, NW
Washington, DC 20410
(202) 512-0000
http://www.access.gpo.gov
　　The GPO publishes over 30,000 booklets, pamphlets, books, and other documents. If there is a particular subject you're interested in, write to the GPO at the address given above. They will send you a list of their publications. Or you can search their catalogs online at the URL above.

JUDICIAL BRANCH

Supreme Court of the United States
U.S. Supreme Court Bldg.
1 First Street, NE
Washington, DC 20543
(202) 479-3000, (202) 479-3011
Public Information Office: (202) 497-3211
  The federal court that settles disputes of
  national importance; also hears appealed
  cases from lower courts.

U.S. Court of Appeals for the Federal Circuit
717 Madison Place, NW
Washington, DC 20439
(202) 633-6550
  Handles cases that have been disputed in
  lower courts.

U.S. District Courts
333 Constitution Ave., NW
Washington, DC 20001
(202) 273-0555
http://www.uscourts.gov
  Trial courts with general federal jurisdic-
  tion. Each state has at least one district
  court.

Federal Judicial Center
1 Columbus Circle, NE
Washington, DC 20002-80003
(202) 273-4000
http://www.fjc.gov
  Researches operation of U.S. courts for
  the public.

OTHER SOURCES OF INFORMATION ON THE U.S. GOVERNMENT

For a wealth of information on the United
States government—its offices, depart-
ments, agencies, and services—see the latest edition of *Information USA* by Matthew
Lesko (Penguin Books, current edition).

There's no shortage of information on
the U.S. government online. Besides the
official government sites listed in this chapter, you might want to check out some of
the following sites provided by other organizations:

Federal Web Locator
*http://www.law.vill.edu/Fed-Agency/
fedwebloc.html#fedjuris*
  An index of federal government
  resources maintained by the Villanova
  Center for Information Law and Policy

Project Vote Smart
http://www.vote-smart.org
  This national, nonpartisan nonprofit
  organization provides a comprehensive
  database that tracks both state and federal government candidates and elected
  officials. Find out who your representatives are, what committees they serve on,
  how they stand on issues you care about.
  Track the status of legislation or find
  links to other sources of information on
  important issues. A free printed guide,
  the *Vote Smart Web YellowPages,* is available free by calling the Voter's Research
  Hotline at 1-800-622-SMAR(T).

Cornell Law School's Legal Information Institute (LII)
http://www.law.cornell.edu/lii.table.html
  LII has created an extensive Web site
  that covers the Supreme Court, including
  biographical information on current jus-
  tices, key decisions of the Supreme
  Court, and court rules.

C-SPAN
http://www.c-span.org/index.html
  C-SPAN offers government information
  online.

CONTACT GROUPS
FOR INFORMATION, NETWORKING, AND PROGRAMS

This section includes listings for many national groups. Contact them for more information, and for addresses of local chapters or groups.

This is not intended to be a comprehensive directory. Check your library reference desk for additional references. Also see:

- **Directories in Print** (Gale Research, updated annually). A listing of all directories available—chamber of commerce directories, buyers' guides, career opportunities, transportation, Christmas decorations—you name it!

- **Directory of American Youth Organizations: A Guide to 500 Clubs, Groups, Troops, Teams,** **Societies, Lodges, and More for Young People** by Judith B. Erickson (Free Spirit Publishing, updated every two years). Lists organizations for peace and global understanding, service groups, political and patriotic organizations, and conservation and humane education groups, among many others. All are adult-sponsored, nonprofit, and national in scope.

- **The Encyclopedia of Associations** (Gale Research, updated annually). This directory of clubs, service groups, and organizations is updated several times a year. Regional versions are now available which list several states in one volume.

IMPORTANT

Before joining any club, group, or organization, check it out carefully. Make sure it represents your values and ideals. Get your parents involved in your decision.

YOUTH CLUBS PROVIDING OPPORTUNITIES FOR SOCIAL ACTION

Boy Scouts of America
1325 West Walnut Hill Lane
PO Box 152079
Irving, TX 75015-2079
(972) 580-2000
http://www.bsa.scouting.org/
> Contact for names and locations of local groups. Builds character, citizenship, and service.

Boys & Girls Clubs of America
1230 Peachtree Street, NW
Atlanta, GA 30309
(404) 815-5789
http://www.bgca.org/
> Youth development and service. Programs and services for youth ages 6–18.

Camp Fire Boys and Girls
4601 Madison Ave.
Kansas City, MO 64112-1278
(816) 756-1950
http://www.campfire.org
> Serves girls and boys. Encourages self-reliance and good citizenship.

Co-Ette Club
2020 West Chicago Blvd.
Detroit, MI 48206
(313) 867-0880
> Leadership training and community service for high school girls. Programs emphasize national and local charitable, civic, educational, and cultural causes. Operations are mostly in the Detroit area.

4-H Youth Development
CFREES/Family Youth Development
U.S. Department of Agriculture
1400 Independence Ave., SW, Room 3905
Washington, DC 20250
(202) 720-2908
http://www.4H-usa.org/
> Coeducational program for ages 8–19. Leadership development. Interest in nation's food and fiber agricultural systems and the family.

Future Farmers of America (FFA)
5632 Mt. Vernon Memorial Highway
PO Box 15160
Alexandria, VA 22309-0160
(703) 360-3600
> Check with state or high school organizations for awards programs.

Girl Scouts of the USA
420 Fifth Ave.
New York, NY 10018
(212) 852-8000
http://www.girlscouts.org/
> Development of individual potential, values, and contributions to society.

Girls Inc.
30 East 33rd Street
New York, NY 10016
(212) 689-3700
http://www.girlsinc.org
> Youth development and service. Serves girls ages 6–18.

National Association of Youth Clubs
5808 16th Street, NW
Washington, DC 20011
(202) 726-2044
> Clubs for boys and girls 8–18, emphasizing character development and community service.

YMCA of the USA

101 North Wacker Drive
Chicago, IL 60606
(312) 977-0031; (800) USA-YMCA
http://www.ymca.net/
> Youth programs that emphasize year-round development.

YWCA of the USA

350 Fifth Ave., Suite 301
New York, NY 10118
(212) 273-7800
http://www.ymca.org/
> Offers youth opportunites for personal growth and self-development, education, health, and fitness.

ANIMAL WELFARE GROUPS

American Society for the Prevention of Cruelty to Animals (ASPCA)

Education Department
424 East 92nd Street
New York, NY 10128
(212) 876-7700
education@uspca.org
http://www.aspca.org/
> Educational materials on humane treatment of animals.

Humane Society of the United States

2100 L Street, NW
Washington, DC 20037
(202) 452-1100
http://www.hsus.org/
> Promotes the humane treatment of animals and "respect, understanding, and compassion for all creatures."

People for the Ethical Treatment of Animals

501 Front Street
Norfolk, VA 23510
(757) 622-7382
http://www.peta-online.org/
> Information on fair treatment of animals. Has free literature for young people on animal rights issues, including companion animal care, vegetarianism, dissection, and helping animals.

Student Action Corps for Animals

PO Box 15588
Washington, DC 20003
(202) 543-8983
> Seeks to empower high school students to work for animal rights movement.

ENVIRONMENTAL GROUPS

Acid Rain Foundation

1410 Varsity Drive
Raleigh, NC 27606
(919) 828-9443
> Educational materials for K–12.

Adopt-A-Stream Foundation

PO Box 5558
Everett, WA 98201
(206) 388-3487
> Guidelines for adopting a stream or wetland. Send a self-addressed, stamped envelope (SASE) and a small donation, if possible.

American Oceans Campaign

235 Pennsylvania Ave., SE
Washington, DC 20003
(202) 544-3526
> Information on protecting the ocean habitat.

American Council for an Energy-Efficient Economy
1001 Connecticut Avenue, NW, Suite 801
Washington, DC 20036
  Free, complete list of energy information sources for youth.

Center for Clean Air Policy
444 North Capitol Street
Suite 602
Washington, DC 20001
(202) 624-7709
  Publishes technical reports on clean air issues, including acid rain, global warming, and toxins.

The Center for Environmental Education
http://www.teachgreen.org
  This database for environmental information and resources has links to other environmental education sites.

Center for Health, Enviroment, and Justice
PO Box 6806
Falls Church, VA 22040
(703) 237-2249
  Several handbooks and "how-to" information.

Cousteau Society
870 Greenbrier Circle
Suite 402
Chesapeake, VA 23320
  Environmental education information.

Defenders of Wildlife
1101 Fourteenth Street, NW
Suite 1400
Washington, DC 20005
(202) 682-1331
http://www.defenders.org/index.html
  Offers free information on biodiversity and threatened and endangered species.

Earth Force
1908 Mount Vernon Ave., 2nd floor
Alexandria, VA 22301
(703) 299-9400
  Town meetings, Pennies for the Planet, and other campaigns. This is a youth-driven organization.

Earth Train
99 Brookwood
Orinda, CA 94563
(510) 254-9101
  Youth teaching youth in a cross-country environmental train and international projects.

Earthwatch
680 Mount Auburn Street, Box 403
Watertown, MA 02272
(617) 926-8200
http://www.gaia.earthwatch.org/
  Recruits volunteers for field research expeditions (archeology to zoology). Ages 16 and older. Operates in 36 countries and U.S.

EcoNet
18 DeBoom Street
San Francisco, CA 94107
(415) 442-0220
http://www.igc.org/igc/econet/
  Serves organizations and individuals working for environmental preservation.

Environmental Defense Fund
http://www.edf.org/
  Works to integrate economic and environmental goals in dealing with environmental problems.

EnviroLink Library
http://www.envirolink.org/EviroLink_Library
  Contains an index of nearly 200 organizations, lists of environmental conferences, and other links.

Friends of the Earth
1025 Vermont Ave., NW
Suite 300
Washington, DC 20005
http://www.foe.org/
(202) 783-7400
A national nonprofit organization that works to protect the environment and preserve biological, cultural, and ethnic diversity.

Global ReLeaf Program
American Forests
PO Box 2000
Washington, DC 20013
1-800-368-5748, (202) 955-4500
http://www.amfor.org/
Environmental education information.

Greenpeace
1436 U Street, NW
Washington, DC 20009
(202) 462-1177
http://www.greenpeace.org/
Environmental education information and advocacy.

Institute for Environmental Education
18554 Hoskins Road
Chagrin Falls, OH 44023
(216) 543-7303
Environmental studies program.

Keep America Beautiful, Inc.
9 West Broad Street
Stamford, CT 06902
(203) 323-8987
http://www.kab.org/
Information on solid waste management and litter prevention.

Kids Against Pollution (KAP)
PO Box 22
Newport, NY 13416
(315) 891-3288
kap@borg.com
A kids' networking group working to fight pollution.

Kids for a Clean Environment (KidsFACE)
PO Box 158254
Nashville, TN 37215
1-800-952-3223
kidsface@mindspring.com
Kids environmental action group. Sends out newsletter.

Kids for Saving Earth Worldwide (KSE)
PO Box 421118
Plymouth, MN 55442
(612) 559-1234
kseww@aol.com
Kids environmental action club. Sends out newsletter.

National Arbor Day Foundation
100 Arbor Ave.
Nebraska City, NE 68410
(402) 474-5655
Join organization and receive free seedlings. Also information on trees.

National Association for Humane and Environmental Education
67 Salem Road
East Haddam, CT 06423
(203) 434-8666
Information on *Kind News* newspaper.

National Coalition Against the Misuse of Pesticides
701 E Street, SE, Suite 200
Washington, DC 20003
(202) 543-5450
Information on alternatives to pesticides.

National Audubon Society
700 Broadway
New York, NY 10003
(212) 979-3000
http://www.audubon.org
Information on organizing youth groups in environmental education.

National Energy Information Center
EI-231, Energy Information Administration
Room 1F-048, Forrestal Bldg.
1000 Independence Ave., SW
Washington, DC 20595
(202) 586-8800
Information on energy.

National Geographic Kids Network
1145 17th Street, NW
Washington, DC 20036
(202) 856-7000
http://nationalgeographic.com.
A telecommunications-based science curriculum for sharing environmental data. Fourth through sixth grades.

National Solid Waste Management Association
1730 Rhode Island Ave., NW
Suite 1000
Washington, DC 20036
(202) 659-4613
Information on recycling and solid waste management.

National Wildlife Federation
Correspondence Division
8925 Leesburg Pike
Vienna, VA 22184
(202) 797-6800
http://www.nwf.org/nwf
Educational materials on wildlife and endangered species.

Natural Guard
142 Howard Ave.
New Haven, CT 06519
(203) 787-0229
tng@snet.net
Works with inner-city kids in community action.

Natural Resources Defense Council
Public Education Department
40 West 20th Street
New York, NY 10011
(212) 727-2700
Information on citizen education and action.

The Nature Conservancy
1815 North Lynn Street
Arlington, VA 22209
1-800-628-6860
http://www.tnc.org
Their mission is to preserve the diversity of life on Earth by protecting natural lands. Call to learn how to adopt an acre of rainforest for free.

Rainforest Alliance
270 Lafayette Street
Suite 512
New York, NY 10012
(212) 941-1900
Information on saving rainforests.

Save America's Forests
4 Library Court, SE
Washington, DC 20003
A nationwide activist effort working for U.S. forest ecosystem protection through legislation. They lobby, organize efforts, raise money for forest causes.

Sierra Club
730 Polk Street
San Francisco, CA 94109
(415) 776-2211
http://www.sierraclub.org
Environmental information. Ask about Inner City Outings, wilderness adventures.

Sierra Student Coalition
145 Waterman St.
Providence, RI 02906
(401) 861-6012
ssc-info@ssc.org
Runs campaigns on public land, clean air, and corporate responsibility.

Student Conservation Association
PO Box 550
Charlestown, NH 03603
(603) 543-1700
National and local community service programs with opportunities in conservation involving youth and adult volunteers.

Touch American Project

U.S. Forest Service
PO Box 96090
Washington, DC 20090
(703) 235-8855
http://www.fs.fed.us/
Volunteer conservation program on public lands for ages 14–17.

United Nations Environment Program (UNEP)

Liaison Office
DC1 Bldg.-590
1 U.N. Plaza
New York, NY 10017
(212) 963-4931
Information on Youth Environment Forum, environmental education.

U.S. Environmental Protection Agency

Office of Environmental Education
Coordinator of Youth programs (A-107)
401 M Street, SW
Washington, DC 20460
(202) 260-8749
http://www.epa.gov/
Environmental education materials for K–12, (202) 260-7751; grant information, (202) 260-4484

U.S. Fish and Wildlife Service

Department of the Interior
18th and C Streets, NW
Washington, DC 20240
(202) 208-5634
http://www.fws.gov/
Information on endangered species and how to conserve fish and wildlife in their natural habitats.

Izaac Walton League of America

707 Conservation Lane
Gaithersburg, MD 20878-2983
(301) 548-0150
Information regarding protection of natural resources.

World Wildlife Fund

1250 24th Street, NW
Washington, DC 20037
(202) 293-4800
Information on protection of endangered wildlife; wetlands; rainforests in Asia, Latin America, Africa.

Youth for Environmental Sanity (YES!)

706 Frederick Street
Santa Cruz, CA 95062
(408) 459-9344
Fax: (408) 458-0255
http://yesworld.org/
Offers World Leadership Camps for youth and multimedia environmental programming to schools.

CIVIC ORGANIZATIONS

American Bar Association

Division for Public Education
541 North Fairbands Court
Chicago, IL 60611-3314
(312) 988-5735
http://www.abanet.org/
Information on the law and civic education. Offers a catalog of publications.

The American Promise

http://www.pbs.org/ap/
The Web site for the television series includes a Community Action Guide featuring stories, local heroes, resources; a Teacher's Tune-In Guide for class activities, discussions. Companion book and video available. Ages 13 and up. To order, call 1-800-358-3000.

Anti-Defamation League (ADL)

823 United Nations Plaza
New York, NY 10017
(212) 490-2525
http://www.adl.org/
Endeavors to stop the defamation of the Jewish people and to secure justice and fair treatment to all citizens alike.

Center for Civic Education
5146 Douglas Fir Road
Calabasas, CA 91302-1467
1-800-350-4223
http://www.civiced.org
   Provides newsletter and educational
   materials on civic education.

Civic Practices Network
http://www.cpn.org
   Brings together many different organizations and perspectives for active citizenship.

Constitutional Rights Foundation
601 South Kingsley Drive
Los Angeles, CA 90005
(213) 487-5590
http://www.crs-usa.org
   This nonpartisan educational foundation
   promotes citizen involvement in government and sends out a newsletter on law-
   related topics.

Corporation for National Service
1201 New York Avenue, NW
Washington, DC 20525
(202) 606-5000
http://www.cns.gov/
   National program in all states that provides money for service programs (K-12),
   AmeriCorps, and other service opportunities.

Electronic Frontier Foundation
http://www.eff.org/
   A popular site. A nonprofit civil liberties
   organization working to protect free-
   doms. Check out their Blue Ribbon
   Campaign for online freedom of speech,
   press, and association:
   http://www.eff.org/blueribbon.html

Frontlash
815 16th Street, NW
Washington, DC 20006
(202) 7893-3993
   High school and college students. Labor
   movement and social progress. Support
   group of the AFL-CIO.

Girls State/Girls Nation—
Boys State/Boys Nation
Contact your state American Legion
Headquarters.
http://www.legion-aux.org
   A model government program for high
   school juniors chosen by their local
   American legion posts to help young people learn about political processes and
   how state and local governments work.
   Two representatives from each state program are chosen to attend a week-long
   study of federal government held in
   Washington, D.C.

HandsNet
http://www.handsnet.org
   National organization that promotes
   information sharing, collaboration, and
   advocacy among people and organizations working on a broad range of public
   interest issues.

Institute for Global Communications
http://www.igc.org/
   Home to PeaceNet, EcoNet, LaborNet,
   ConflictNet. Each is a gateway to articles, headlines, features, and links.

Junior Statesmen of America
60 East Third Ave., Suite 320
San Mateo, CA 94401
1-800-334-5353
   Prepares young leaders for participation
   in democratic self-government.

Kids Voting USA
398 South Mill Avenue, Suite 304
Tempe, AZ 85281
(602) 921-3727
http://www.kidsvotingusa.org/
A national organization that supplies
educational kits and encourages kids to
vote with their parents at the polls

National Association for the Advancement of Colored People (NAACP)
Washington Bureau
1025 Vermont Avenue, NW, Suite 1120
Washington, DC 20005
(202) 638-2269
http://www.naacp.org/
Works for political, educational, social,
and economic equality of minority group
citizens of the United States.

National Organization for Women (NOW)
1000 16th Street, NW, Suite 700
Washington, DC 20036
(202) 331-0066
http://www.now.org/
Strives to eliminate discrimination and
harassment in the workplace, schools,
and the justice system, eradicate racism
and sexism, and promote equality and
justice in society.

National Teen Age Republican Headquarters
PO Box 1896
Manassas, VA 22110
(703) 368-4214
Principles of free enterprise, constitutional government, patriotism. STARS groups
for 9–12 years old.

National Youth Leadership Council
1910 West County Road B
Roseville, MN 55113
(612) 631-3672
http://www.nylc.org
A repository of service projects and ideas.

People's Anti War Mobilization
1470 Irving Street, NW
Washington, DC 20010
(202) 332-5041
High school and college students who
oppose war, imperialism, racism, discrimination.

Street Law, Inc.
918 16th Street, NW, Suite 602
Washington, DC 20006-2902
(202) 293-0088
Information on law-related education
grades 6-12. (Formerly National Institute
for Citizenship Education and the Law.)

Webactive
http://www.webactive.com/
A weekly online publication that helps
activists to find other organizations and
individuals with similar values and interests.

Who Cares
PO Box 3000
Denville, NJ 07834
1-800-628-1692
http://www.whocares.org/
A quarterly journal devoted to community service and social activism, available
by subscription or online.

Young Americans for Freedom
14018-A Sullyfield Circle
Chantilly, VA 22021
(703) 378-1178
Conservative political youth organization
promoting free enterprise, national
defense, etc. Ages 14–39.

Young Democrats of America
c/o Democratic National Committee
430 South Capitol Street, SE
Washington, DC 20003
(202) 863-8000
http://www.democrats.org
Fosters aims of the Democratic Party for
ages 18–30.

Youth as Resources

1700 K Street, NW, Suite 801
Washington, DC 20006
(202) 466-6272, ext. 131
http://www.yar.org/
 Information and support for youth service.

Youth Service America

1101 15th Street, NW
Washington, DC 20005
http://www.servenet.org/ysanet2/index.html
 Information and support for youth service.

INTERNATIONAL GROUPS

AFS International Intercultural Programs

198 Madison Ave., 8th Floor
New York, NY 10016
1-800-237-4636
http://www.afs.org/us
 Promotes international exchange of high school students in over 60 countries. May live with host families. Volunteer work included.

Amnesty International Youth Program

1118 22nd Street, NW
Washington, DC 20037
(202) 775-5161
http://www.amnesty.org/
 The oldest, biggest human rights organization in the world, and one of the most respected.

CARE

151 Ellis Street NE
Atlanta, GA 30303-2439
1-800-521-CARE or 1-800-277-3025
http://www.care.org/
 Worldwide organization that assists the world's poor in their efforts to achieve social and economic well-being. Programs include emergency relief and food aid.

Children of War

Religious Task Force
85 South Oxford Street
Brooklyn, NY 11217
(718) 858-6882
 International peace leadership program for ages 13–18. Membership from 13 countries. Designed to counter racism and violence among youth.

Children's Campaign for Nuclear Disarmament

14 Everit Street
New Haven, CT 06511
(203) 226-3694
 Completely youth-run organization. Ages 18 and younger. Dedicated to ending the arms race.

Council on International Education Exchange

205 East 42nd Street
New York, NY 10017
(212) 661-1414
 Volunteer service programs at high school and college levels. Information on over 200 opportunities for study, adventures, worldwide travel for ages 12–18.

Global Kids Inc.

http://www.slc.edu/alumnaei/alumpages/lrhoades/FINALWEB.HTML
 A resource page for young people and a chance to speak out.

Human Rights Watch

485 Fifth Avenue
New York, NY 10017-6104
(212) 972-8400
http://www.hrw.org/
 This coalition of human rights groups attracts the best researchers in the field.

Human Rights Web

http://www.hrweb.org/
 Up-to-date information about human rights with links to organizations. Includes "Getting Started: A Primer for New Human Rights Activists."

International Christian Youth Exchange

134 West 26th Street
New York, NY 10001
(212) 206-7307

International experiences for ages 16–35 in 32 countries.

International Pen Friends

Box 290065
Brooklyn, NY 11229-0001

Headquartered in Dublin, Ireland, this group can connect you with 250,000 pen pals of all ages in 153 countries. Send a self-addressed, stamped envelope (SASE) for information.

Kids Meeting Kids

380 Riverside Drive
New York, NY 10025
(212) 662-2327

Organization of kids ages 5–19 from around the world which promotes peace, fair treatment of young people, and a better world. Send SASE for information.

Model UN (United Nations)

UN Association of the USA
485 Fifth Ave.
New York, NY 10017-6104
(212) 697-3232

Opportunities for young people to participate in model United Nations and youth programs.

Open Door Student Exchange

250 Fulton Ave.
PO Box 71
Hempstead, NY 11551
(516) 486-7330

International educational exchange organization. High school students and families. Scholarships available.

PeaceNet

18 DeBoom Street
San Francisco, CA 94107
(415) 441-0220
http://www.igc.org/igc/peacenet/

International computer-based communication system for promotion of peace.

University of Minnesota Human Rights Library

http://www.umn.edu/humanrts/

Excellent source for human rights documents. Includes the Universal Declaration of Human Rights, Declaration of the Rights of the Child, and many more. Also additional links.

World Future Society

7910 Woodmont Ave., Suite 450
Bethesda, MD 20814
(301) 656-8274
http://www.wfs.org/wfs

Promotes study of the future. Draws from U.S. and 80 countries. Serves as clearinghouse for information about the future.

World Learning

Kipling Road
Brattleboro, VT 05301
(802) 257-7751
http://www.worldlearning.org

Citizen exchange, language instruction, international development and training. Summer home stays for high school students and young adults.

SOCIAL ACTIVISM AND SOCIAL ISSUES

Action

1100 Vermont Ave., NW
Washington, DC 20525
(800) 424-8867

Student Community Service Program,
Volunteers in Service to America (VISTA),
Foster Grandparent, Action Drug Alliance
(which provides funding/seed money for
local substance abuse education and prevention).

Activism 2000 Project

PO Box E
Kensington, MD 20895
1-800-KID POWER
(301) 929-8808
(301) 929-8907 fax
ACTIVISM@aol.com

This national clearinghouse encourages
young people to be pragmatic idealists
and community problem solvers.

American Red Cross

Program and Services Department
Youth Associate
431 18th Street, NW
Washington, DC 20006
(202) 639-3039
http://www.redcross.org/

Encourages volunteerism, leadership
development, community involvement.
Opportunities in disaster services, health
and safety services, HIV and AIDS education, and international services. Online,
go to "Youth" for information on ages 25
and under.

America's PRIDE Program

National Parents' Resource Institute for
Drug Education
3610 Dekalb Technology Parkway
Atlanta, GA 30340
(770) 458-9900
http://www.prideusa.org

Offers a range of drug prevention programs and services to young people, parents, community organizations, and
schools.

Big Brothers/Big Sisters of America

230 North 13th Street
Philadelphia, PA 19107
(215) 567-7000
http://www.bbbsa.org/

Adult volunteers aid youth in problems
of drug abuse, teen pregnancy, foster
care, juvenile delinquency, sexual abuse,
etc.

Child Welfare League of America

440 First Street, NW, 3rd Floor
Washington, DC 20001
(202) 638-2952
http://www.cwla.org/

National network of youth programs
focusing on youth as trainers for teen
pregnancy prevention, quality parenting,
self-sufficiency.

Childhelp USA

6463 Independence Ave.
Woodland Hills, CA 91367
1-800-4-A-Child

Child abuse prevention, information,
counseling, contacts, hotline

Close Up Foundation

44 Canal Center Plaza
Alexandria, VA 22314
(703) 706-3300

A program that gives kids a close-up look
at how government works, teaching civic
responsibility and social action. Also has
educational materials.

Educators for Social Responsibility

23 Garden Street
Cambridge, MA 02138
(617) 492-1764

Information about how to involve your teachers in creating new ways of education for active and responsible participation in the world.

Guardian Angels

Junior Guardian Angels
982 East 89th Street
Brooklyn, NY 11236-3911
(718) 649-2607, (212) 397-7822

Trains volunteers to seek to deter crime through unarmed street patrols. Over 50 participating cities. Junior Angels for ages 11–15.

Habitat for Humanity International

121 Habitat Street
Americus, GA 31709
(912) 924-6935
http://www.habitat.org/

Works to provide affordable housing and eliminate poor housing and homelessness worldwide.

National Clearinghouse for Alcohol and Drug Information

PO Box 2345
Rockville, MD 20847
(800) 729-6686, (301) 468-2600
http://www.health.org/

A federal clearinghouse for information and educational materials for drug and alcohol abuse prevention.

National Collaboration for Youth

1319 F Street, NW, Suite 601
Washington, DC 20004
(202) 347-2080

Consortium of 15 major voluntary youth-service organizations. Advocates needs of youth in substance abuse, youth employment, juvenile justice, etc.

National Crime Prevention Council

1700 K Street, NW, 2nd Floor
Washington, DC 20006-3817
(202) 466-6272
http://www.ncpc.org/

Information on fighting crime. Request a copy of the "Neighborhood Watch Organizers Guide," read it online.

National Network of Runaway and Youth Services, Inc.

1319 F Street, NW, Suite 401
Washington, DC 20004
(202) 783-7949

Network of services for youth, including delinquency, drug use, adolescent pregnancy prevention, crisis intervention, independent living, family therapy, etc. Direction and training for youth.

National Self-Help Clearinghouse

25 West 43rd Street, Room 620
New York, NY 10036
(212) 642-2944

Provides information and referral to self-help groups throughout the country. How to organize your own groups.

Planned Parenthood Federation of America

810 Seventh Ave.
New York, NY 10019
(212) 541-7800
http://www.plannedparenthood.org

Information on teen pregnancy prevention.

Serve America (National Service Commission)

529 14th Street, NW, Suite 452
Washington, DC 20045
(202) 724-0600

Information on state directors for youth service, and service learning.

Special Olympics, International
1350 New York Ave., NW, Suite 500
Washington, DC 20005
(202) 628-3630
    Information on Special Olympics.

Students Against Destructive Decisions (SADD)
PO Box 800
Marlboro, MA 01752
    Student organization founded to combat drunk driving and underage drinking. Its expanded mission addresses issues of poor decision-making and risk-taking such as violence, suicide, sexually transmitted diseases, and binge-drinking.

Volunteers of America, Inc.
110 South Union Street
Alexandria, VA 22314
(703) 548-2288
http://www.voa.org
    Wide range of youth services and volunteer opportunities.

AWARDS AND RECOGNITION FOR KIDS

Many national groups recognize kids who have made contributions in their communities. Some award you with certificates or trophies; other offer cash prizes or expenses-paid trips to receive the award. Contact them by mail or phone to find out specifics. If you ask at your local youth, church, school groups, city and state agencies, you will probably discover additional award possibilities.

For more information on awards check your library reference desk for *Awards, Honors, and Prizes*, Vol. 1, U.S. and Canada (Gale Research, current edition).

Albert Schweitzer Institute for Humanities—Environmental Youth Awards
PO Box 550
Wallingford, CT 06492
(203) 697-2744
Awards celebrating environmental activism and awareness by students ages 12-18

America the Beautiful Fund
1511 K Street, NW, Suite 611
Washington, DC 20005
(202) 638-1649
http://www.americashmall.com
Administers Operation Green Plant, a national recognition program for projects utilizing free seed packets.

American Health Care Association
Public Relations Office
1201 L Street, NW
Washington, DC 20005-4014
(202) 842-4444
Teen Volunteer of the Year awards for volunteer work in nursing homes. Nominated by state Health Care Association. Awards plaque, gift, and expenses-paid trip to convention. Ages 13–19.

American Red Cross
National Office of Volunteers
Attention: Awards and Recognitions
811 Gatehouse Road
Falls Church, VA 22042-1203
(703) 206-7410
Offers School and Community Award for Youth in Health and Safety and presents the Woodrow Wilson Award to a youth under 21 for contributions to the Red Cross and community. Nomination by chapters.

The Bayer/NSF Award for Community Innovation
1-800-291-6020
http://www.nsf.gov/bayer-nsf-award.htm
Student teams submit proposals for improving the quality of life in their communities, using the scientific method to develop a solution to a community problem. Bayer Corporation and the National Science Foundation offer more than $50,000 in grants and savings bonds to winning teams. Grades 6–8.

Boys & Girls Clubs of America
1230 W. Peachtree Street, NW
Atlanta, GA 30309
(404)815-5700
Offers many awards, including the Golden Youth Awards for local service and the National Youth of the Year Award for outstanding contributions to home, school, church, community, and boys/girls clubs. Local, state, regional winners. National winners receive a scholarship sponsored by *Reader's Digest*. Ages 12–18.

Brick Award

Do Something
423 West 55th Street, 8th Floor
New York, NY 10019
(212) 523-1175
http://www.dosomething.org/brickwhat/
  Awards grants of $10,000 (for continuing community service) to ten outstanding young Americans under age 30. Grand prize winner $100,000.

Chevron Conservation Awards Program

575 Market Street, Room 870
San Francisco, CA 94105
(415) 894-6083
http://www.chevron.com
  Annual conservation awards of $1,000 in three categories: citizen volunteers, professional conservationists, and nonprofit conservation organizations.

Colgate Youth of America Award

PO Box 1058, FDR Station
New York, NY 10150-1058
(212) 736-0564
  Open to Boy Scouts/Girl Scouts, Boys Clubs/Girls Clubs, Camp Fire, and 4-H Clubs. Forty-three prizes.

Congressional Award Foundation

PO Box 77440
Washington, DC 20013
(202) 226-0130
  Recognizes youth for voluntary public service and personal excellence. Bronze, silver, gold medals. Ages 14–23.

EF Ambassador Scholarship

EF Center Boston
One Education Street
Cambridge, MA 02141
(617) 252-6000
(617) 621-1930 fax
  Awards a free educational tour of Europe to one student (grades 9-12) from each U.S. state and Canadian province, based on applicants' proposals to change the world, either at a local or global level.

ExploraVision Awards

Toshiba/National Science Teachers Association
1840 Wilson Blvd.
Arlington, VA 22201-3000
(703) 243-7100
1-800-EXPLOR+9
http://www.nsta.org/programs/explora.htm
  Students K-12 work in teams to envision what a form of technology might look like in 20 years.

Freedoms Foundation at Valley Forge

Route 23, 1601 Valley Forge Rd.
Valley Forge, PA 19482
(610) 933-8825
ffvf@ffvf.org
  National awards for schools, individuals, organizations for promoting responsible citizenship.

Future Farmers of America (FFA)

5632 Mt. Vernon Memorial Highway
PO Box 15160
Alexandria, VA 22309-0160
(703) 360-3600
  Recognitions through high school chapters for community service, safety activities, agriculture awards, etc.

Future Problem Solving Program (FPSP)

2500 Packard Rd., Suite 110
Ann Arbor, MI 48104-6287
1-800-256-1499
http://www.fpsp.org
  Sponsors an annual awards competition for Community Problem Solving/Future Problem Solving for those registered in FPSP. Individual deadlines for affiliates. Community Problem Solving national competition. Winners go to international competition.

The Giraffe Project
PO Box 759
Langley, WA 98260
(360) 221-7989
http://www.giraffe.org/giraffe/
Recognizes courage of individuals of all ages who "stick their necks out" for others. Also offers training in community action.

Girl Scouts/Boy Scouts/4-H Clubs, etc.
Check local chapters for awards and recognitions.

International Juvenile Officer's Association
7 Lake Ave.
Saratoga Springs, NY 12866-2210
Gives the Joseph G. Phelan Award to honor a youth for outstanding service in delinquency prevention and control.

Jefferson Awards/*Weekly Reader*
American Institute for Public Service
621 Delaware Street, Suite 300
Newcastle, DE 19720
(302) 323-9116
info@aips.org
http://www.dca.net/clients/aips
Sponsored by *Weekly Reader* for outstanding public service. Annual awards. State winners receive Jefferson Award, medal, and expenses-paid trip (with chaperon) to Washington, D.C.

Joint Action in Community Service
5225 Wisconsin Ave., Suite 404
Washington, DC 20015
(202) 537-0996
1-800-522-7773
Awards for community volunteer work.

Keep America Beautiful, Inc.
Awards Program Coordinator
9 West Broad Street
Stamford, CT 06902
(203) 323-8987
keepamerbe@aol.com
http://www.kab.org
Annual awards to youth and school groups for environmental improvement, litter prevention, beautification, recycling, etc. Presentation of awards in Washington, D.C.

National Arbor Day Foundation
Awards Committee
100 Arbor Ave.
Nebraska City, NE 68410
(402) 474-5655
http://www.arborday.org
Offers awards to individuals and schools for work in tree planting, stewardship, or education.

National Association for the Advancement of Colored People (NAACP)
Check local branches for awards and recognitions.

National Safe Kids Campaign
America Challenge
Scholastic, Inc.
555 Broadway
New York, NY 10012-3999
(212) 505-4962
Dedicated to safety and prevention of unintentional childhood injury. They host 50 awards to youth and an advisor, who are flown to Washington, D.C., to receive award. Awards are for safety programs and projects.

National Wildlife Federation
National Conservation Awards Program
8925 Leesburg Pike
Vienna, VA 22184
(202) 797-6800
http://www.nwf.org/nwf
Annual awards for contributions to the
environment. Awards statuette of
whooping crane and expenses-paid
trip to receive award.

Parents Without Partners International Information Center
401 North Michigan Ave.
Chicago, IL 60611-4267
(312) 644-6610
Youth of the Year Award for children of
members involved in family, school, or
community projects.

J.C. Penney—Golden Rule Awards
PO Box 10001
Dallas, TX 75301
(214) 431-1000
Presents a National Youth Award for
volunteer service in community. Local
award winner receive bronze sculpture;
the agency associated with youth
receives $2,000. The national award is
a bronze medallion, and the agency
receives $5,000; youth receives $5,000
scholarship. Ages 18 and under.

A Pledge and a Promise Environmental Awards
Sea World
7007 Sea World Drive
Orlando, FL 32821
SeaWorld@bev.net
Anheuser-Busch Theme Parks distribute
13 environmental stewardship awards
for K—college. Large cash awards for
running your environmental project.

Points of Light Foundation
1737 H Street, NW
Washington, DC 20006
(202) 223-9186 ext. 202
volnet@aol.com
The President's Service Award is given
for outstanding community service.
Ceremony at the White House.

President's Environmental Youth Awards
Coordinator for Youth Programs A-107
401 M Street, SW
Washington, DC 20460
(202) 260-8749
Ten regional winners and sponsor receive
expenses-paid trip to Washington, DC, to
receive annual awards for contributions
to environment. Corporate sponsorships
and grants to winners.

Prudential Spirit of Community Awards
National Association of Secondary School
Principals (NASSP)
http://www.prudential.com/community
Honors middle and high school students
for volunteer community service.

Reebok Human Rights Programs
100 Technology Center Drive
Stoughton, MA 02072
(617) 341-5000
(617) 341-4377
karen.hirschfeld@reebok.com
http://www.reebok.com
Youth-In-Action Award for contributions
to human rights. Donates $25,000 to a
human rights organization designated by
the recipient.

Religious Heritage of America
1750 South Brentwood Blvd., Suite 502
St. Louis, MO 63144-1315
(314) 962-0001
1-800-325-3016
Youth awards for service, leadership in
church, school, community. Awarded trip
to RHA weekend conference.

Renew America

1400 Sixteenth Street, NW, Suite 710
Washington, DC 20036
(202) 232-2252
1-800-922-7363
renewamerica@igc.apc.org
http://www.crest.org/renew_america
National awards for environmental sustainability.

U.S. Department of Justice Programs

Young American Medals Committee
633 Indiana Ave., NW
Washington, DC 20531
(202) 307-0703
http://www.usdoj.gov
Awards the Young American Medal for Bravery and the Young American Medal for Service for outstanding character and community service. Ages 18 and under. Nominations must come from state governors. Awards expenses-paid trip to Washington, D.C., to receive medal.

Windstar Youth Award

2317 Snowmass Creed Road
Snowmass, CO 81654
(303) 927-4777
Annual scholarship award for youth who shows leadership in environmental action.

Yoshiyama Award

PO Box 19247
Washington, DC 20036
(202) 457-0588
Awards $5,000 to six to eight high school seniors for extraordinary community service.

Youth Earth Service Awards

300 East 56th Street, 14G
New York, NY 10022
Celebrates and awards youth earth service.

Part 5

TOOLS

BRAINSTORMING 1: COME UP WITH IDEAS

Idea - Ideas **That makes me think of:** **More WILD & crazy ideas—keep going**

At this point, you have many ideas, some of them crazy. Now you should choose an idea to work on.

Ask yourself questions. *Examples:* Which idea might benefit the most people? Which idea might have the best chance to succeed? Which idea might cost the least to do? Which idea might make the biggest difference? Which idea do I like the best?

Think of questions which will help you make a good choice.

Questions

1. _____
2. _____
3. _____
4. _____
5. _____

Choose one basic idea to work with:

_____

Now list the steps to carry out your Plan of Action. *Examples:* Give speeches at the Community Council; write letters to the mayor; write a news release for TV and radio.

Then write down who will be responsible for each step, and when.

Plan of Action

	Activity	Who Does It?	When
1.			
2.			
3.			
4.			
5.			
6.			
7.			

(Use another sheet of paper if you need more space)

Reproduce this form for each person who offers suggestions.

Name of contact: _____

Title: _____

Company/organization name: _____

Street address: _____

City, State, ZIP code: _____

Phone number: _____

Email address: _____

Web site: _____

How can this person or organization help you find a solution or help you carry out your solution?

_____

_____

_____

_____

_____

_____

_____

_____

_____

_____

_____

_____

"Hello. May I please speak to _____ **or someone in public
relations or public information?"**
(contact's name)

"My name is _____ **and I'm from your school/grade/organization."**
(your name)

1. Purpose (what you're going to say or ask): _____

_____

_____

_____

_____

_____

2. Information (write down what your contact tells you): _____

_____

_____

_____

_____

_____

(Attach more paper if you need it.)

"Thank you very much."

- -

Date of call   Your name

School/group phone   School/group address

Contact's name   Title

Contact's phone   Contact's address

Name of your school or group
Home, school, or group street address
City, State, ZIP code

Date

Name of person you are writing to
Title of person you are writing to
Name of newspaper, office, or company
Street address
City, State, ZIP code

Dear (Name of person you are writing to):

(Indent the beginning of each paragraph, if you wish.)

Sincerely,

Your Name
Your Grade

_____

_____

_____

_____

_____

_____

_____

_____

_____

_____:

_____

_____

_____

_____

_____

_____

_____

_____

_____

FAX COVER SHEET

To: _____

Company: _____

Fax number: _____ Business phone: _____

From: _____

School or organization: _____

Fax number: _____

School or organization phone: _____

Date: _____

Number of pages (including this one): _____

Subject: _____

_____

_____

_____

_____

_____

_____

_____

_____

_____

_____

_____

INTERVIEW FORM

In Person _____
By Phone _____
By Letter _____

Name of person interviewed

Title

Phone number

Company/organization name

Street address

City, State, ZIP code

Email address

Date of interview

From: _____ To: _____
Time   Time

Questions

1. _____

2. _____

3. _____

4. _____

5. _____

(Write the answers to your questions on a separate sheet. Make sure you number your answers the same as the questions.)

Your name

Your school/grade/organization

You can use this survey form to record one person's responses to your survey.

Write a question after each number. Record responses (SA = Strongly Agree, A = Agree, D = Disagree, SD = Strongly Disagree, U = Undecided) on the shorter lines to the left of the numbers.

_____ **1.** _____

_____

_____ **2.** _____

_____

_____ **3.** _____

_____

_____ **4.** _____

_____

_____ **5.** _____

_____

_____ **6.** _____

_____

_____ **7.** _____

_____

_____ **8.** _____

_____

_____ **9.** _____

_____

_____ **10.** _____

_____

This survey form can be used to tally many people's responses to your survey.

Statements or Questions

1. _____
   _____

2. _____
   _____

3. _____
   _____

4. _____
   _____

5. _____
   _____

Responses

SA = Strongly Agree   A = Agree   D = Disagree   SD = Strongly Disagree   U = Undecided

	SA	A	D	SD	U
1.	*				
2.					
3.					
4.					
5.					

*Mark a line for each response (┼┼┼).

TABULATION OF SURVEY RESULTS

	SA	A	D	SD	U
1.	*				
2.					
3.					
4.					
5.					
6.					
7.					
8.					
9.					
10.					

SA = Strongly Agree   A = Agree   D = Disagree   SD = Strongly Disagree   U = Undecided

*Write the number of people who strongly agree with question #1.

COMMENTS: _____

_____

_____

_____

_____

PETITION

_____
(Title of Petition)

A Petition of: _____
(your group or organization)

Addressed to: _____

We, the undersigned, would like to bring your attention to the following problem, with recommendation(s):

_____

_____

_____

Agreed upon by the following people:

	Name	Address/Group/School	Phone
1.			
2.			
3.			
4.			
5.			
6.			
7.			
8.			
9.			
10.			
11.			
12.			
13.			
14.			
15.			

_____
(Title of Proposal)

Presented to: _____

Presented by: _____

Date: _____ School or organization: _____

Description of Proposal:

_____

_____

_____

Organizational Plan

_____

_____

_____

Needs:

_____

_____

_____

Budget:

_____

_____

_____

Time Line:

_____

_____

_____

Most grant applications ask you to provide the following information (some ask for even more). Check off each item as you complete it.

____ **1.** Write a statement that explains your problem. Include strong facts and perhaps a story to support your statement.

____ **2.** Describe your goals. Tell how your project will help to solve your problems. How will it improve on what has already been done by others?

____ **3.** Describe your project.

____ **4.** Tell how long you think your project will take.

____ **5.** Tell how you plan to achieve your goals. Describe your method or list the steps you will take.

____ **6.** Include a budget (how much money you will need, and how you plan to spend it). Include a list of what you think your expenses might be. Include any donations of time and materials you hope to receive.

____ **7.** Tell how you plan to evaluate your progress—how you will show that you are achieving your goals.

____ **8.** Tell how your project might benefit the grantors (the organization or foundation you are asking to give you a grant). They like compliments as much as you do. For example, is there any way you can advertise that they funded your project?

____ **9.** If you want to make your grant application stand out from the rest, you might try using charts, graphs, videos, slides, audiotapes, or other creative ideas . How about a splash of color?

____ **10.** Keep a copy of your grant application, in case the grantors lose the original. (It happens.)

____ **11.** Send your application by registered mail. You will get a receipt saying that it has been received. Or, if possible, hand-carry it into the grantors' office.

____ **12.** Follow up your application with letters, phone calls, or personal visits. Be persistent but polite. This will let the grantors know that you're serious about your request.

____ **13.** If you receive your grant, be sure to send thank-you notes to your grantors (and anyone else who helped you to win your grant).

____ **14.** You will probably be required to write a follow-up report. If so, be sure to do it!

____ **15.** If you don't receive your grant, request an evaluation from the grantors explaining their reasons for refusing your application. You'll learn important pointers you can use in future grant applications.

Contact:

For Immediate Release

_____
Name

_____
Address

_____
City, State, ZIP code

_____
Phone

_____
Date

_____
Email

WHAT _____
_____

WHO _____
_____

WHEN _____
_____

WHERE _____
_____
_____

DETAILS _____
_____
_____
_____
_____
_____

Name of your group

Address

City, State, ZIP code

Target Audience

Beginning Date

Ending Date

Contact Person

Phone

Email

Topic

TEXT

Number of seconds

Number of words

END

PROCLAMATION

WHEREAS, _____

_____

_____

_____, and

WHEREAS, _____

_____

_____

_____, and

WHEREAS, _____

_____

_____

_____ .

Now, therefore, be it

RESOLVED, _____

_____

_____

_____ .

Signed this _____ **day of** _____

_____   _____

_____   _____

_____   _____

_____   _____

VOTER REGISTRATION (DOOR-TO-DOOR CAMPAIGN)

1. Hello, my name is _____ **and**

(name)

I'm from _____ .

(your school or group)

I am supporting _____ .

(your candidate or issue)

2. Would you please tell me if you are registered to vote?

❑ YES, registered

❑ NO, not registered

_____

Name

_____

Address of house or apartment

If the answer is YES, leave literature and thank the person.

If the answer is NO, do one of the following:

_____ (a) Register the resident in the Registration Book

_____ (b) Leave a mail-in registration form

_____ (c) Inform the resident of neighborhood registration:

_____

Date(s)

_____

Location(s)

_____

Phone number of local voter registration office

3. Thank the resident, and once again ask for support for your candidate or issue.

4. Comments from residents, or additional information:

_____

_____

_____

Excuse me, please. May I talk with you for a moment?

My name is ———————————————— **, and I'm representing kids from**
(name)

———————————————————————————————— .
(your school or group)

1. **Would you please vote for (or against)** ———————————————— **?**
(number & name of bill)

2. **This is important because** (Give you "needs" statement—your reasons for supporting or opposing the bill.)

———————————————————————————————

———————————————————————————————

3. **Our solution is** (Tell how supporting or opposing the bill would help your cause.)

———————————————————————————————

———————————————————————————————

4. **Do you have any questions or suggestions?** (Write down any questions or suggestions the legislator has.)

———————————————————————————————

———————————————————————————————

5. **May I please have your support?** ❑ YES ❑ NO ❑ MAYBE

6. **Thank you very much for your time.**

——————————————————— ———————————————
Legislator's name Date

———————————————————
Your name

——————————————————— ———————————————
Group Phone (group)

———————————————————————————————
Address (school/group/hometown)

———————————————————————————————
Your legislative district

———————————————————————————————
Names of your legislators

LOBBYING BY PHONE

Hello. May I please speak to _____ **or a legislative assistant?**
(legislator's name)

My name is _____ **, and I'm from**
(name)

_____ .
(your school or group)

1. Would you please vote for/against _____ **?**
(number & name of bill)

2. This is important because (Give your "needs" statement—your reasons for supporting or opposing the bill.)

_____

_____

3. Our solution is (Tell how supporting or opposing the bill would help your cause.)

_____

_____

4. Do you have any questions or suggestions? (Write down any questions or suggestions the legislator has.)

_____

_____

5. May I please have your support?   ❑ YES   ❑ NO   ❑ MAYBE

6. Thank you very much for your time.

If the legislator isn't there, leave a message with the secretary: your name, school or group, phone number, school or group address, hometown, title and number of proposed bill, and how you want the legislator to vote.

Legislator's name _____   Phone _____

Email _____   Address _____

City, State, ZIP code _____

Which committees has the legislator served on? _____

Date _____   Your name _____

Group _____   Phone (group) _____

Address (school/group/hometown) _____

Your legislative district _____   Names of your legislators _____

My name is _____ , and I'm from

(name)

_____ .

(school or group)

Thank you for this opportunity. We would also like to thank our sponsor,

_____ **for giving us valuable help.**

(name of sponsor)

1. We would like to encourage you to support (or oppose):

_____

Number & name of bill or measure

2. This is important because (Give your "needs" statement—your reasons for support-ing or opposing the bill. Include a quote, statistic, or example.)

_____

_____

_____

3. We believe the best solution is (Tell how supporting or opposing the bill would help your cause.)

_____

_____

(Tell how you have worked with your opposition):

_____

_____

(Tell who supports your position):

_____

_____

4. Do you have any questions or suggestions?

_____

_____

5. Thank you for your time. We would like to ask you for your support.

_____

_____

1. **WHEREAS,** The _____
_____
_____
_____, and

2. **WHEREAS,** The _____
_____
_____
_____, and

3. **WHEREAS,** The _____
_____
_____
_____, therefore be it

4. **RESOLVED,** That _____
_____
_____
_____, and be it further

5. **RESOLVED,** That _____
_____
_____
_____, and be it finally

6. **RESOLVED,** That _____
_____
_____
_____.

STUDENT COURT CHART

Student name

Grade

Homeroom

Date rule was broken

Rule that was broken

Consequences for breaking the rule

Date for completion of consequences

Date of follow-up appearance at student court

I understand the rule that I broke and accept the consequences determined by the court. I agree to complete the consequences and appear before the student court again on the date listed above.

Student's signature

Judge's signature

Sponsor's signature

BIBLIOGRAPHY

Book of the States, Lexington, KY: The Council of State Governments, 1996–97.

Broadcasting/Cable Yearbook, Washington, D.C., 1997.

A Citizen's Guide to Community Education on Global Issues, Sherry Rockey and Alice L. Hughey, Washington, D.C.: League of Women Voters Education Fund, 1988.

Civic Writing in the Classroom, Sandra Stotsky, Bloomington, IN: ERIC Clearinghouse for Social Studies/Social Science Education, 1987.

The Congressional Record, Washington, D.C.: U.S. Government Printing Office, printed daily; April 27, 1989, E 1407; May 27, 1988, S 7129.

The Constitution of the United States, various editions.

Creative Action Book, Sydney Parnes and Alex Osbourne, New York: Scribners, 1962.

Democracy at Work: A Study of Utah's Election Laws and Procedures, for the League of Women Voters, Bountiful, UT: Carr Printing Company, 1985.

Directory of American Youth Organizations: A Resource Guide to 500 Clubs, Groups, Troops, Teams, Societies, Lodges, and More for Young People, Judith B. Erickson, Minneapolis, MN: Free Spirit Publishing Inc., 1998–1999 edition.

How Our Laws Are Made, Washington, D.C.: U.S. Government Printing Office, Doc. No. 99-158, 1986.

If You Want Air Time: A Publicity Handbook, Jane Freundel Levey, Washington, D.C.: National Association of Broadcasters, 1987.

Making an Issue of It: The Campaign Handbook, Washington, D.C.: League of Women Voters, 1976.

The Municipal Year Book, Washington, D.C.: International City Management Association.

A Sourcebook for Creative Thinking, Sydney Parnes and Alex Osbourne, New York: Scribners, 1962.

The State of the States, Scott Ridley, Washington, D.C.: Fund for Renewable Energy and the Environment, 1987.

Tell It to Washington: A Guide for Citizen Action, Washington, D.C.: League of Women Voters Education Fund, Pub. No. 349, 1987–88.

The United States Government Manual, Washington, D.C.: U.S. Government Printing Office, 1997–98.

INDEX

ABOUT THE AUTHOR

Barbara A. Lewis is a national award-winning author and educator who teaches kids how to think and solve real problems. Her students at Jackson Elementary School in Salt Lake City, Utah, have worked to clean up hazardous waste, improve sidewalks, plant thousands of trees, and fight crime. They have instigated and pushed through several laws in their state legislature and an amendment to a national law, garnering 10 national awards, including two President's Environmental Youth Awards, the Arbor Day Award, the Renew America Award, and A Pledge and a Promise Environmental Award. They have also been recognized in the *Congressional Record* three times.

Barbara has been featured in many national magazines, newspapers, and news programs, including *Newsweek, The Wall Street Journal, Family Circle,* "CBS This Morning," "CBS World News," and CNN. She has also written many articles and short stories for national magazines. Her other books for Free Spirit Publishing— *Kids with Courage, The Kid's Guide to Service Projects,* and *What Do You Stand For? A Kid's Guide to Building Character*— have won many national awards.

Barbara has lived in Indiana, New Jersey, Switzerland, and Belgium. She and her husband, Larry, currently reside in Park City, Utah. They have four children: Mike, Andrea, Chris, and Sam.

Other Books from Free Spirit

The Kid's Guide to Service Projects
Over 500 Service Ideas for
Young People Who Want
to Make a Difference
by Barbara A. Lewis

Hundreds of ideas for all kinds of service projects, from simple ones anyone can do to large-scale commitments that involve whole communities. Ages 10 and up.

$10.95; 184 pp.; softcover; 6" x 9";
ISBN 0-915793-82-2

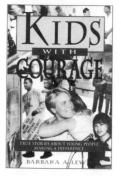

Kids with Courage
True Stories About Young People
Making a Difference
by Barbara A. Lewis

Eighteen remarkable kids speak out, fight back, come to the rescue, and stand up for their beliefs. These true stories prove that anyone, at any age, in any life circumstance, can make a real difference in the world. Ages 11 and up.

$10.95; 184 pp.; softcover; B&W photos;
6" x 9"; ISBN 0-915793-39-3

What Do You Stand For?
A Kid's Guide to Building Character
by Barbara A. Lewis

This book empowers children and teens to identify and build character traits. Inspiring quotations, background information, dilemmas, activities, true stories, and resources make this book timely, comprehensive, thought-provoking, and fun. Ages 11 and up.

$18.95; 280 pp.; softcover; B&W photos
& illus.; 8½" x 11"; ISBN 1-57542-029-5

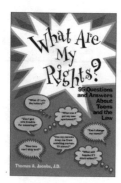

What Are My Rights?
95 Questions and Answers About
Teens and the Law
by Thomas A. Jacobs, J.D.

Teens need to know about the laws that affect them—so they can make informed decisions about what they should and should not do. This fascinating book helps teens understand the law, recognize their responsibilities, and appreciate their rights. Ages 12 and up.

$14.95; 208 pp.; softcover; 6" x 9";
ISBN 1-57542-028-7

Girls and Young Women Leading the Way
20 True Stories About Leadership
*by Frances A. Karnes, Ph.D.,
and Suzanne M. Bean, Ph.D.*

First-person stories by girls and young women prove that anyone can be a leader, regardless of gender or age. Ages 11 and up.

$11.95; 168 pp.; softcover; B&W photos;
6" x 9"; ISBN 0-915793-52-0

The Ultimate Kids' Club Book
How to Organize, Find Members,
Run Meetings, Raise Money,
Handle Problems, and Much More!
by Melissa Maupin

Everything kids want and need to know to start and run a successful club of any type or size, for any reason, anywhere: at home, at school, in a community center, or place of worship. Ages 10-14.

$11.95; 120 pp.; softcover; illus.; 6" x 9";
ISBN 1-57542-007-4

Fighting Invisible Tigers
A Stress Management Guide for Teens
Revised and Updated Edition
by Earl Hipp

Proven, practical advice for teens on coping with stress, being assertive, building relationships, taking risks, making decisions, dealing with fears, and more. A perennial bestseller. Ages 11 and up.

$10.95; 160 pp.; softcover; illus.;
6" x 9"; ISBN 0-915793-80-6

1998–1999 Directory of American Youth Organizations (7th Edition)
A Resource Guide to 500 Clubs,
Groups, Troops, Teams, Societies,
Lodges, and More for Young People
by Judith B. Erickson, Ph.D.

The most comprehensive guide available to adult-sponsored, nonprofit youth organizations in the United States, the *Directory* points young people toward hundreds of possibilities for fun, friendship, social action, and self-esteem. Ages 6-18 and youth workers.

$21.95; 200 pp.; softcover; 7" x 10";
ISBN 1-57542-034-1

*To place an order or to request a free catalog of SELF-HELP FOR KIDS®
materials, please write, call, email, or visit our Web site:*

Free Spirit Publishing Inc.
400 First Avenue North • Suite 616 • Minneapolis, MN 55401-1724
toll-free 1.800.735.7323 • local 612.338.2068 • fax 612.337.5050
help4kids@freespirit.com • www.freespirit.com